Ruth Markel was born in M[...] Masters Degree in Social W[...] management and organizat[...] [...]ing at post-graduate level. As a consultant, entrepreneur and lecturer, she has given seminars for business women in Canada and many other countries. She lives in Toronto, Canada, with her husband and two children.

Carolyn Faulder took her degree in philosophy as the mother of three small children and remembers the experience as the hardest job of her life. She has always worked, and as a journalist has found that her two abiding interests – health issues and career opportunities for women – have coincided with an exciting, endlessly evolving period of social change. Her books include *Cosmopolitan's Careers Guide*, written out of her experience of setting up and running a careers advisory service for readers of *Cosmopolitan* magazine.

MOVING UP

A Woman's Guide
to a Better Future at Work

RUTH MARKEL
and
CAROLYN FAULDER

Fontana/Collins

First published in Canada under the title *Room at the Top* 1985
First published in Great Britain in 1988 by Fontana Paperbacks
8 Grafton Street, London W1X 3LA
Second impression June 1988

Set in Linotron Sabon
Printed and bound in Great Britain by
William Collins Sons & Co. Ltd, Glasgow

CONTENTS

ACKNOWLEDGEMENTS

I am grateful to Helen, my mother, who offered me a rich variety of examples and taught me the power of principle and determination; and to Phil, Shelly and Danny for their constant support.

I would like to thank my daughter, Clemencia Faulder, for the help she has given me in preparing the British edition of this book. She has done painstaking research and carried out many in-depth interviews. Above all, I have appreciated her useful and always constructive critical comments, based on her front-line experience of moving up in the world of work.

INTRODUCTION

This is a book for women who are serious about their work but light-hearted about life. They want to enjoy everything – their job, themselves and their personal relationships. They want to succeed, but on their terms, and for some, but not all of them, that will mean coming out on top. They know that work is for living and that a career doesn't just happen, it has to be made.

Whatever their particular ambitions, the last thing such women want is to turn into imitation men. Yet they realize that if they are going to take up a strong, respected position in the marketplace they must learn the existing rules before they can adapt them to their own needs.

All the strategies, skills and tips you need to achieve these aims are described in detail within these pages. There is a basic career plan here for every working woman, no matter what her status or experience. But it isn't good enough to be told how it is; the best learning is by doing and that is the unique value of this book.

Ruth Markel wrote the original version which was published in Canada in 1985 under the title *Room at the Top*. It has since been published in both France and Germany and has helped many women in the world of work. This revised and updated edition is based on her long experience of running workshops and seminars for business and professional women, and is packed with questionnaires to set you thinking about who you are and what you really want to do. There are also worksheets in every chapter to help you plan your career future.

Take your time going through the book. We suggest you take copies of both questionnaires and worksheets and keep them, with your answers, in a loose-leaf file. This will enable you to check your progress and see how well you are meeting the goals you set yourself.

We have also included plenty of real-life examples – successes and failures – to illustrate problems, and ways of solving them, as well as mistakes to avoid. We are grateful to these women who were willing to give up so much time to talk frankly about their working experiences and whose stories bring this book alive.

You may not want to put everything into action straightaway but you should be aware that at some time in your career you will have to face the issues covered in this book. There are steps, there are formulas for getting there, there are pay-offs and there are setbacks, but basically you are in charge of your own destiny.

Think of what you learn from this book as a secret rocket you tuck into your pocket. When the time comes for your career to take off you will be ready to press the button and soar.

CAROLYN FAULDER
London, 1987

The Work Turning Point

Women have always been in the work force. In pre-industrial times their contribution to the family breadbasket was significant and recognized, but when industrialization moved labour from the fields and the hearth into the newly created factories and offices, the majority of women were left behind to care for home and family. It was still work they did – and hard indeed it was in those days before labour-saving devices were available – but because it wasn't paid, it was given no value.

It is only in the last twenty years that women have begun to enter in droves the outside labour market. There are many reasons for this: economic need; changing attitudes; higher expectations – both material and spiritual; more women becoming better educated; and, not least, a growing conviction in the community at large that it is more than a matter of social justice – it makes sound economic sense to draw on all the talents and resources that are available within the population.

We all have different reasons for taking up paid employment. Money is the most obvious and, if work is available, most people want to earn their living rather than be dependent on another or on the State. Although money is important – and women in particular should beware of underestimating the value of that commodity – it's not usually the sole reason why we want to work.

For some women the economic factor can play second fiddle to less concrete but no less important factors like job satisfaction; a desire for recognition; getting a buzz from feeling that you are making a worthwhile contribution to society; or, in the case of women especially, a need to create an identity distinct from being someone else's wife or mother. Married women, whatever their social or economic position, are no longer prepared to retire from the workplace once they start a family. They have enjoyed a spell of economic independence; they have appreciated the freedom and sense of self-worth it has given them and they don't want to relinquish these advantages for ever. Certainly, they may wish to take a few years off while their children are small, but, once the children have started school, most women are raring to get back into employment.

A large number of women don't, of course, have the luxury of being able to choose whether they wish to work. A job, congenial or not, part-time or full-time, is a necessity, particularly in areas of high unemployment where the men are likely to be the first to be laid off.

The family unit is no longer what it was. Twenty years ago approximately 20 per cent of households consisted of father as breadwinner, mother as housewife and their 2.5 children. Today only 5 per cent of households conform to this pattern. The following figures serve to underline the changing social scene in Great Britain.

11 million women in Britain are economically active.

42 per cent of the work force is female, the second highest proportion in Europe (after Denmark).

64 per cent of married women work.

68 per cent of non-married women work.

51 per cent of mothers with dependent children work.

48 per cent of working women work part time.

830,000 single-parent families are headed by the mother, 89.2 per cent of the total number.

Whoever you are, we will take it as read that money and what it can buy you, whether it is a pressing obligation to pay the bills, a short-term 'luxury' goal such as buying a new car or nice clothes, or a longer-term commitment like contributing to the mortgage repayments, constitutes a major motivation for working. But it is not the only one and the longer you are employed the more likely it is that you will be seeking other rewards from your work.

Understanding why you work and where you want your work to take you is crucial to getting the most out of a job. When you start asking yourself questions like: *Do I enjoy my work? Am I getting the rewards I deserve? And if not, why not?* Or, more fundamentally, *Should I be in this job at all? And if not, what am I going to do about it?* you will realize that you have reached a turning point in your career or work history. This is a life crisis just like any other and you will probably encounter the work crisis more than once. To resolve it positively you must prepare yourself to confront it as a challenge rather than as a threat to the status quo.

Later we shall be helping you to find out the answers to these and many other questions so that when you come to your own particular work turning point you can be sure of taking the right road forward. But first we will start by examining more closely exactly how much time we devote to our work.

Diagram 1a is designed to help you observe how your job fits into your total life style; it may surprise you to see how much of your time is spent working.

Diagram 1a

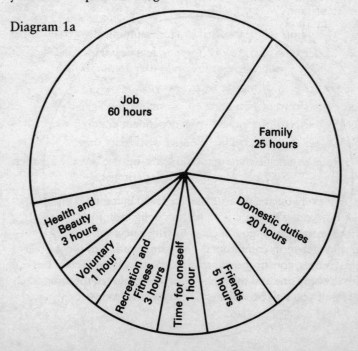

Valerie is marketing manager in a company making toys and games. She is married and has two teenage children. Diagram 1a shows a breakdown of a typical week in her life. Each segment of the circle represents an interest or activity in her week. There are 168 hours in a seven-day week and Valerie gets by on about seven hours of sleep a night.

After looking at it, examine your own life and the amount of time you give to the same activities:

Job
Family
Friends
Domestic duties
Time for yourself
Beauty and hygiene
Exercise
Travel
Interests (hobbies, voluntary work, etc.)

Diagram 1b

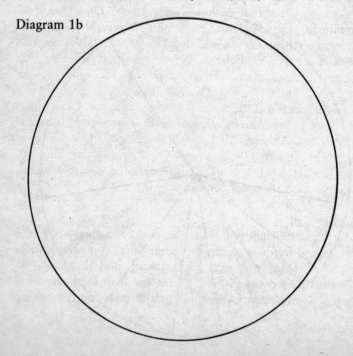

Now mark out the blank circle in Diagram 1b into segments, the size of each corresponding to the time consumed by each of the above activities.

You may be surprised to find that half, possibly even more, of your time is spent working. In other words, work is central to most of us in our lives. And yet, how many of us plan our jobs – both short-term and long-term – with anything like the same attention and concern we show our families and friends?

Given that a job will occupy most of us for such a significant portion of our lives, it's important to stand back and take a long look at what we are actually doing during those hours of work. Although many women still kid themselves that they are only working to achieve short-term goals, in fact it's very likely that their employment outside the home will become a long-term part of their lives. Once they accept that, they will begin to ask themselves questions like: *How do I make the most of my job? How can I make it grow? How can I make my working hours more worthwhile to me?*

Once a woman accepts that she is not just working at a temporary job, but that she has become involved in a long-term commitment, she will start to think a little bigger. She will begin to want more from her job – responsibility, pay, status, freedom and a richer existence. But before she reaches that point, she will undergo a period of transition and crisis – the work turning point.

Consider, in this context, the following examples. Cathy, Joan and Sandra are three women from completely different backgrounds. Although they are different ages and working in quite different areas, there is one thing they all share: they are going through a work crisis. Each woman has a particular job problem which she must confront.

Cathy

Cathy is twenty-eight years old. She works as a secretary to the marketing director in a large multinational company. She is married to Don, who is a civil servant, and they have no children. Cathy earns £10,000 a year and their joint income is over £30,000 a year. Cathy and Don have just moved from a one-bedroom flat into a renovated Victorian terrace house in a newly gentrified area of London. They each have their own car.

Although Cathy is not very happy in her job, she knows she must work to maintain the life style she and Don have made for themselves. Their new house represents a big investment but they have no intention of giving up such pleasures as the theatre, eating out, entertaining friends and taking good holidays. Moreover, Cathy still wants to be able to buy smart, therefore expensive, clothes when she needs them.

At the moment Cathy is working purely for short-term goals, but, if she wants to maintain her life style, she will be forced to re-evaluate her job. How can she turn it into a career? How can she switch from short-term, easily achieved goals to making longer-term, more complex plans? Cathy needs a bit of a push because she has never really thought about the fact that she will probably work for most of her adult life. In many ways, she is going through the everyday motions with her eyes closed.

Cathy is a victim of *complacency*.

Joan

Joan is fifty-two. She returned to work ten years ago to help pay for holidays, clothes, extra tuition and all the other expenses of three teenage children. Her husband, Bill, owns his own carpet-cleaning business and they live comfortably in their mortgage-free home in a country town.

Their children are now out of college and no longer need financial help. Bill is planning to retire and Joan thinks he will want her to spend more time with him. Since the children are now independent and Bill will have a good pension, there is no longer quite the same financial need for Joan to work. However, she enjoys her job in the personnel department of a medium-sized manufacturing company and she doesn't want to give it up. Recently, the position of office manager became vacant and, because the company is known to prefer hiring from within, Joan is fairly certain that she has a good chance of being offered the job.

Before she makes any decision, Joan must re-evaluate and analyse her commitment to her work. If she accepts the new position, she will have to deal with the shift of personal responsibility from her family to her career.

Joan is facing a *dilemma*.

Sandra

Sandra is thirty-three. She has a science degree and always intended to have a career. Now divorced (she married a fellow student straight out of university), she has no qualms about the world of work. Self-confident and quietly assertive, she has made steady progress and currently holds a job in sales in a paper manufacturing company. She supervises a staff of eleven and regularly makes high-level presentations to corporate managers throughout the country.

Sandra is aware that there is only one way forward and that is *up*, but she has an Achilles heel to contend with – her unadmitted fear of success. She doesn't like the idea of entering into the political arena of top management. The competition scares her and she is afraid that she will be cut off from her staff. She believes she could be reasonably happy staying put in her present position but she does like money and what it buys. She also knows she works best when she's faced with a challenge, but, if she's going to make this bid for top management, she's going to have to acquire a new approach and the skills necessary for advancement.

Sandra is experiencing *frustration*.

Cathy, Joan and Sandra are all experiencing work crises that will force them to take a hard look at their priorities. In so doing they will all confront their goals, both short-term and long-term.

All three women are facing a work turning point. Cathy has a job; she must begin to think about a career. Joan must decide between remaining in the comfortable niche where her career takes second place to a family that no longer needs her in the same way, or readjusting her past priorities to accept new challenges. Sandra is committed to change. Even so, she must get rid of some psychological baggage before she will be able to move ahead with alacrity. She also needs to make a comprehensive career plan and acquire some further skills in order to equip her for greater management responsibility.

Much has been written about the personal or life crisis in its various forms. Depending on the way you meet it, it can either be an upsetting and unproductive experience which fails to resolve anything, or, it can push you to open your eyes and facilitate solutions which lead you into a better situation.

Writers such as Erik H. Erickson, author of *Childhood and Society*, Daniel Levinson, author of *The Seasons of a Man's Life*, and Gail Sheehy, author of *Passages*, all describe a series of personal crises which tend to occur at fairly specific times in people's lives. The work crisis is a little different because it has no recognizable chronological form and it can reappear in a different guise more than once.

Women who may have started work with only short-term goals in view often develop habits and aspirations which lead them to look for more than the pound in their pocket. They enjoy the power that economic independence gives them and then they begin to want more: they demand job satisfaction, they seek out new horizons and they realize they must plan ahead. This means they must seek promotion within the company for which they presently work, or go elsewhere.

As you have now discovered from working out your own Diagram 1b, you probably spend *more* time on your job than on any other single activity. Yet you may be spending proportionately *less* time thinking about it than you do about other activities – for instance, the chores. There are several reasons why many women are still slow to develop a long-term perspective about their work:

1. We have been socialized to believe that creating a home and bringing up a family is a sufficient and respectable life plan that should fulfil any woman. This process starts in the home, carries on at school and is often perpetuated in our adult life by other women as well as by husbands.

2. Wanting children and deciding when to have them inevitably disrupts a woman's working life.

3. Most women consider their husband's needs and careers

18

before their own; some work only part time so that they can deal with children and housework; others give up their job when their husbands are relocated or retire.

4. Women often seek out very flexible short-term arrangements in order to balance family and work plans. Inevitably, this means they can't be offered promotion or more responsibility.

5. In times of family pressure and stress, one of the first solutions for a woman is to reduce the time she spends working.

While the above factors are still important and will remain relevant to our perception of work for some time to come, in many ways they are old history. To a great extent they reflect society's inadequate adaptation to the growing presence of women in the workplace and, more important still, their rising expectations.

Many women want it all – husband, children and a satisfying career – and why not? Men have never had this problem – and of course they have usually been helped by having supportive wives. Until we succeed in forcing a fundamental change in work patterns, these are still going to be considerations that women can't ignore. There have been, however, some dramatic changes in the last five years which have helped precipitate a quite specific work crisis for many working women. The subtitle of this book could well be *There Is No Going Home*.

Defining the turning point

The work crisis as we have defined it may accompany other life situations or critical events, and it can occur at any time. Briefly, a work crisis occurs when a woman recognizes and accepts certain facts about her position as a paid employee, many of which she may never have acknowledged before. This flash of recognition often induces confusion and a sense of frustration followed by a period of transition.

The major factors in a work crisis are as follows:

1. *Work is no longer a substitute for something else*. There are still many women who have been brought up to believe that they

19

will find their greatest fulfilment in their roles as wives and mothers. Consequently, even if they have trained for a career in, say, nursing or the law, they may, deep down, assign a subsidiary role to their work. The furthest ahead they are prepared to look is to think, somewhat vaguely, that work will always be there to pick up later, after the children. Women who started with less ambition or fewer opportunities are even more likely to look on their job as a stopgap between school and marriage.

Of course, there are many other women, especially those now leaving school or in their twenties or early thirties, who do see work as an integral part of their lives. Nonetheless, they may be feeling trapped because they know they are in the wrong job or aren't sure which career they should be choosing. And then finally there are those other women, further on in their careers, who may have done rather well but now seek a change of direction.

All these women are in a work crisis and they know they are because they are all asking the same important question: *What will I do with the rest of my life?* It is at this point that many women discover for the first time that their work really matters to them. Deep down they know that a job is no longer just a choice, but a necessity. Moreover, a growing number of women are beginning to feel that although interesting work entails responsibility, it also brings rewards and satisfactions which can't be obtained from any other activity.

2. *Your role at work is a vital part of you.* Once a work crisis strikes, you will eventually have to confront the realization that the person you are at work has become inextricably entangled with the person you are in your private life. A very significant *you* – be it executive secretary, television researcher, middle manager or whatever – has begun to demand equal billing with the other roles already familiar to you. Your professional identity has moved into the limelight with your existing roles – daughter, wife, mother, lover, school governor, member of a women's group, or whatever.

You will probably find that this new you, the professional woman, has, without conscious effort, become integrated into your existing life style. It may have begun to show itself in your choice of new friends, the activities you become involved in and the social events you attend. It may also influence your conversation and develop your self-confidence. It's bound to have an effect on your self-presentation; the way you dress, even perhaps the way you speak. But most of all it is a transformation that comes from within.

3. *Am I ready?*
Another aspect of this period of transition is feeling anxious. You will be nervous and worried because you don't think you are well enough prepared to perform the new tasks necessary for success. You may worry that you have no managerial experience, no knowledge of how to read a profit and loss account, no understanding of budgets. . . . There's a distinct possibility that you may be required to speak in public, and the prospect terrifies you.

The first step towards conquering this anxiety is to recognize that your future advancement will probably depend on acquiring some new skills. Once you face this fact you can draw up a plan for getting those you require, either through formal training or informal contacts.

It's important to realize that some of the anxiety involved in a work crisis is not confined to the job itself. By taking on extra responsibilities at work you may be causing some problematic changes in your whole life style. Longer working hours, the prospect of moving to another city or a shift in the balance of economic power if you have a partner, can all involve stressful adjustments in your personal life and relationships.

If you recognize any of these emotions you are probably in the middle of a work crisis. Don't despair. Remember that 'crisis' is another way of saying 'turning point'. Your opportunity for change is at hand, so although your particular work crisis may, for a while, cause you considerable pain, self-doubt and confusion, you can achieve a positive outcome, providing you think out a strategy and handle it in a positive manner. There *is* a way out.

1. *By setting goals.*
A woman who has responded to the growth signals of her work crisis will initiate an organized plan for advancement based on appropriate, realistic goals which are neither too high nor too low.

2. *By developing a strategy for moving up.*
The launch of your professional self-development course should begin as follows:
   i. Take an active approach to your career by making long-term plans.
   ii. Continually review and evaluate your progress.

In the following chapters we will discuss goal-setting in more depth and we will also show you how to develop a long-term career plan which will help you to make progress in the organization or area of work you have chosen. We will also alert you to some of the traps you must be aware of on the way up. The important thing to remember is that if you have recognized that you are experiencing a work crisis, you have already taken the first step. Once you have accepted the necessity of planning for the long term, you're on your way.

Learning to think of your work as an asset will be one of the first changes to emerge from a work crisis. If you start investing in yourself by gaining new skills, according to a long-term plan, you will, over a period of time, increase the value of your abilities.

It's important to realize, however, that you will never be able to rest on your laurels and completely relax. Because the market fluctuates so much in ways that are beyond your control you must constantly take stock of what you have to offer and make improvements that correspond to current market conditions. Unlike gold, you are not a simple, unchangeable commodity. You can adjust and improve your experience and skills rendering you less vulnerable to the whims of the marketplace. Assess your weaknesses and do everything you can to rectify them. Review your strengths and develop them with an eye to what is required for success in the current environment – and in the future.

The importance of a long-term plan will become clear in the following chapters. But before you can begin to think about the future in any significant way, it is essential to have a very good grasp of the here and now. Consequently, we have included at this point a series of questions which are intended to help you evaluate your present position. Not only should they clarify some of your feelings about work; they should also help you to frame your future aspirations in terms of realistic goals.

After you have answered these questions, put them to one side for a week or so. When you return to them they will have been cooking on the back burner, so to speak, and you will probably find that some of your ideas have become clearer. The picture often looks quite different after a fresh look.

Are you ready?

The best way of answering the following questions about yourself is to think ahead – perhaps in periods of twelve-month blocks. Bear in mind that you need a sound understanding of your present status before you can feel secure in your twelve-month plan. This applies *only* to your work.

1. Do you feel your work is optional?

Short-term	(less than twelve months)	Yes □	No □
Long-term	(one to three years minimum)	Yes □	No □

2. Do you have a permanent commitment to working?

Full time	Yes □	No □
Part time	Yes □	No □

If you say 'yes' to either part of the first question, ask yourself if you think that your job is optional forever, or just for the forseeable future. In other words, are there family pressures, economic conditions, etc. that influence the importance you attach to working? Do you feel that work is only a part of your life, just as the weekend is a time for leisure? Can you see yourself doing the same thing for twelve months? If so, are you comfortable with this?

23

When answering the second question, do some critical thinking. Reflect on the possible benefits for you of a twelve-month plan. This exercise is designed to start you thinking on a long-term basis about your work. It may be the first time you have really thought about it in this way.

If you answered 'yes' to working full-time on a permanent basis, you will probably need some tools to help you determine how to plan for advancement more effectively. More about that later.

If you answered 'yes' to working part time, you will want to question yourself concerning the benefit of part-time work to your life style. Is it for money, interest, or to get out of the house? Or is it because that's all the time you can spare or the only type of work you can find? Whatever your answer to these subsidiary questions you will have to consider whether part-time work has a limiting effect on your options. Or is there some way you can make it contribute to your advancement?

After reviewing your answers to the above, the next step is to ask yourself more detailed questions that will help you formulate your goals and see yourself from a new angle, that of a woman whose best assets include her work skills.

Summarizing your work history

It's important to do this summary carefully because it will help you to understand exactly what your work means to you. Don't be deceived by the apparent simplicity of the questions which follow. If you answer them thoughtfully, reflecting on what your past experience tells you about yourself, you will find it a very profitable and illuminating exercise. A useful spin-off from doing this job review is that it will enable you to put together a good CV when the time comes for you to test the water.

1. How many years have you been working?
   Full time:
   Part time:
   Interruptions (children, unemployment, travel, other):

2. i.   Where did you first start working?
   ii. At what level (clerical, business, graduate, professional, etc.)?

3. i.   When you first started working, was it mainly for:
         Economic necessity
         Job satisfaction
         Personal enrichment
         Other (define)
   ii. Do you still work for the same reasons (if not, what are your present reasons)?
   iii. Do you foresee any changes in your reasons for working in the next twelve months (if so, name them)?

4. i.   Have you changed jobs or job levels in the last two years?
   ii. If you have changed either or both, what was the reason for the change?
         Promotion in recognition of good work
         Self-generated
         Being in the right place at the right time (e.g. departure of boss)
         Transfer within the company
         A sideways step
         Other (define)

5. Has a fear of being stereotyped the hard-nosed 'woman boss' ever kept you back?

6. i.   Do you have any children?
   ii. Do you have reservations about being a working mother?
   iii. If so, do you see your children – or your possible decision to have children – as something that's holding you back from being ambitious at work?

We all differ in our perceptions at work. Your answers to these questions will tell you what are the key points to look for when you are making decisions about your work.

For example, what does this review of your work history reveal about your work attitudes? Do you have a tendency to move around? Do you detect a certain consistency in the type of jobs you have done and the satisfaction that you require from them?

How have you answered question 3? You may be surprised at your answers but they will help you to discover your motivations for work. Most of us won't deny that we work for economic necessity, so if you only work for that reason, your twelve-month plan may be to make more money. But should your answer also include a desire for job satisfaction, which is not currently being met, then your plan will have to incorporate finding a job that interests you personally as well as paying you adequately.

Whatever your reasons for working, we can't emphasize enough how important it is for you to know and understand them *now*. Unless you do, you can't make intelligent plans. For instance, if you plan to have children and take time off from work, you will have to build your strategy round that priority. If you have reservations about something such as a fear of being a 'woman boss' or, like Sandra, you are worried about the implications of being very successful, then you must confront these personal dilemmas in order to deal with them.

Diagram 2 indicates some common goals that people have for their careers. It will help you determine the goals which matter to you. Draw your own diagram and put in your own goals, numbering them in the order of importance they have for you. Keep this personal goal diagram with the summary you have made of your work history, and have a look at them both twelve months from now. You may be surprised at some of the changes which have taken place in your attitudes but they will help you to draw up your next twelve-month plan.

Diagram 2

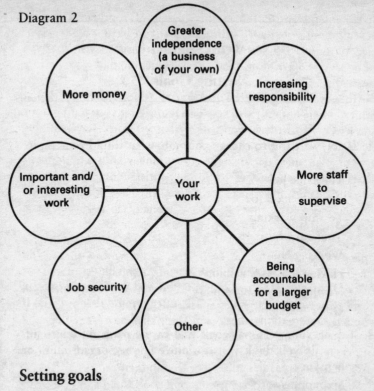

Setting goals

It's one thing to set goals, another to achieve them. If your goal is 'to be happy', then you're not being specific enough. A realistic goal is one that can be achieved within a measurable period and evaluated. 'Happiness' is difficult enough to define, let alone evaluate. Think in terms of simple goals at first – an increase in pay, or greater responsibility in a particular area (e.g., budgets, staff supervision) – and then think of some specific steps you can take to achieve the desired result.

It is also essential to establish a timetable, otherwise you will always be making excuses for yourself. How soon do you want to accomplish your goal? When should you make each step along the way? Can you measure the effectiveness of each step?

All these questions must be taken into account when filling in the following worksheet.

WORKSHEET 1

Setting Goals

1. If you were free to change your job, what would your choice be?

   The same job
   A higher level job
   To stop working
   Your own business
   Working less
   Having less responsibility
   Having more responsibility
   Other (define)

2. Taking your personal goals and career plans into account, where do you think you can move in your organization or sphere in:

   Six months
   One year
   Two years

3. What major goal would you like to achieve in the next twelve months?

4. Work out a step-by-step plan to achieve the goal.

   Step One: Date:
   Step Two: Date:
   Step Three: Date:

Summary

Your work is your own asset – maintain it and develop it
Take a positive approach to your twelve-month plan
Set realistic goals
Evaluate your progress regularly

2

Where Are You?

Janice left school ten years ago with three 'A' levels, in English, French and German. She decided against university because she felt she was not academic enough and trained instead as a bilingual secretary. She had never been encouraged to have high expectations for herself and she assumed that she would work only for a few years before she married and started a family. The job she got in an international chemical company didn't interest her but she worked at it for four years with sufficient competence that she received regular, if somewhat meagre, salary increases.

At that point her long-standing relationship with a man ended. They had been going out together for more than two years but, unlike Janice, he was reluctant to marry and have children. Much put out by this reversal in her private life, Janice went to her boss and pointed out that with her languages she could be doing a more interesting job. Pleased by her initiative, he promoted her soon afterwards to become assistant to the marketing manager.

Although she was qualified for the job on paper, Janice didn't get along with her new colleagues. For starters she was not a team player, a trait that might be tolerable in clerical positions but is absolutely unacceptable at the managerial level. Moreover, she considered herself to be a cut above most of the people with whom she worked and, since she made no effort to conceal this view, it often resulted in behaviour which was downright eccentric.

Six months after accepting her new job, Janice became involved with another man. She began bragging to her colleagues

30

that he was well-to-do and she let them know that once the marriage plans were finalized, she would be quitting her job to live in a style to which she intended to become accustomed. Unfortunately this marriage also fell through.

Her work suffered even more and her job appraisal was not up to scratch. Not only had she alienated most of the people in her department, but her lack of interest in her work was interpreted by her superiors to mean, rightly or wrongly, that she was incompetent. Her boss issued a stern warning that she was under the gun.

The problem for Janice is that she lacks confidence in all areas of her life – private as well as working. She is neither determined enough nor really sure of herself as a competent professional to stay and prove her colleagues wrong. So she is currently looking for another job. Unless, however, her own attitudes and motivations change drastically in the interim, she will arrive at her new position destined to repeat the same mistakes.

Janice's problem, though somewhat extreme, is not unique. She is a woman who lives in the fantasy world that so many women have been brought up to believe in. She is still waiting for her knight in shining armour to come and rescue her from the day-to-day realities of life. She has not matured enough emotionally to realize that this only happens in fairy tales.

Consequently her personal life takes precedence over her career in ways that are self-destructive. She has sacrificed her prospects of developing an interesting career to the short-term gratifications of romance. She has not accepted that her commitment to work is likely to last a lifetime, and, while she obviously wants to achieve the same kind of commitment in a relationship, she has been mistakenly pinning too many of her hopes on another person.

If Janice wants to find more satisfaction in her life she must start by doing some long-term planning for herself and accept positively that work is likely to be a permanent fixture in her life. Like any woman who really wants to advance in her career, she will find that the drive to achieve depends upon the ability to dream – not vapid daydreams but concrete objectives which can be written into a plan for progress.

31

Dreams

'It may be those who do most, dream most.' – *Stephen Leacock*

Before you can move up through your organization, or develop your career in any direction, you must be genuinely committed to advancement – yours. This commitment embraces your vision of the future – and your dreams. Any plans you make will not be worth the paper they are written on unless you have given them this commitment.

The part that dreams play in a career path studded with success can't be overestimated. Our vision of this book is that it should provide guidance and a plan that will help women to put their own dreams into action. Dreams are essential to a long-term plan.

And yet, though we all may dream, the sources of our dreams can be dramatically different. Consider, for instance, the story of one aspiring woman who was interviewed for this book. A member of a family with several generations of achievement to its credit, her drive to be successful was accelerated by this consciousness of her heredity. She wanted to join their ranks.

Another high achiever we talked to was motivated by an equally powerful family-based drive, but of a reverse order. Her parents were immigrants who had experienced a tough time establishing themselves in their new country. She felt that her success fulfilled their own thwarted dreams and justified their struggle.

Try asking yourself what is the source of your dreams, and then, next question, what are those dreams? It seems that few women look for success within their own organization, like, for instance, confidently expecting to become managing director or chairman. They prefer to dream about things external to their present working life, such as doing a world tour, starting their own business or writing a book. But if women intend to develop their careers within a company and generally wish to widen their contribution to business and industry, then their choices, decisions and dreams should be angled to include the reality of making it to the top.

So take a new look at your organization. Getting ahead requires more than time and energy; it needs thinking about, planning for, and lots of careful preparation. But doesn't the prospect of fulfilling some of your career hopes inspire you to dream?

Assessing your current environment

Many women at home are so busy with the exhausting schedule required to manage housework, child rearing and so on that they have no time or energy to think about the future. The same is sometimes true of women at work, particularly those burdened with two jobs because they are looking after a family as well.

If you are serious about advancing, it's vital that you take the time to look around you. No matter how hard you work – or how well – if you always keep your head down to the task in hand you will never be able to see the wider horizon.

The place to begin looking at the larger picture is your current environment. If you have dreams for your career, you must match them to the realities of your working life. Similarly, if you intend to invest a lot of energy in moving up within your organization, you must make sure that that energy will be rewarded.

The following questions are designed to help you determine whether or not your dreams, time and energy will be best invested in your current situation. You may find that trying to advance from your present position is a waste of time. If that's the case, then perhaps you should consider looking for a new job. If, however, you feel that there are opportunities for progress where you are now, your answers will help you to work out the next moves.

1. How many women are there in management positions in your company?

2. How many women have been promoted in the last year?

3. What criteria does your organization use to determine success?

4. How many people are ahead of you?

5. Will it take too much time for them to move?

6. Are there any 'gaps' or new opportunities opening up in your organization?
7. Are you a possible candidate for any of them?

The easier strategy for moving up quickly is to choose an organization in which women have already advanced because this indicates that the company has a positive non-discriminatory employment policy. However, since everyone is now fully aware of the law and an increasing number of companies are anxious to prove that they are 'equal opportunity employers', you should not let an apparent dearth of women managers in a particular company dismay you. If you like everything else about it and think there could be a place in it for you, then have no hesitation in applying. But do remember that because of your sex, you may be treated as a pioneer, and everything tends to be heaped on pioneers – blame as well as praise.

If a full-frontal attack is not to your taste, then the first step in your long-term plan for advancement should be to select an organization with a good track record for employing and promoting women managers. The second step is to take a good hard look at the organization itself – its structure and its objectives. Can you see yourself making a valuable contribution? Can it offer you a position where you will be noticed?

Try to find a company which is diverse and innovative. Stay away from companies that are inbred with rigid patterns or obviously old-fashioned in their attitudes towards women. It's all very well to be impressed by a few women managers scattered around head office but these women may be occupying token positions. Are they the sort of women who look as if they will help their younger sisters coming up behind? The way to get answers to these questions is to ask around.

Depending upon your particular needs, the size of the city or the character of the community in which you live can also be a significant factor. A small town or close-knit community can be beneficial for a particularly talented woman. Her reputation will travel quickly across the business sector. But larger cities offer other benefits: a wider spectrum of opportunities, more openings, better pay and a greater range of contacts, including a chance to tap into existing women's networks.

Look around you. If you don't see good opportunities in your present organization, are there other companies in the area which look interesting? If not, are you willing to move to another part of the country? These questions are all part of that larger picture you must consider if you are seriously thinking about advancement.

Factors that affect advancement

No matter how elaborate your plans for advancement are, you will have great difficulty in getting ahead if you fail to take note of some vital factors that are common to all working situations. Diagram 3 is designed to illustrate the general dynamics underlying most jobs.

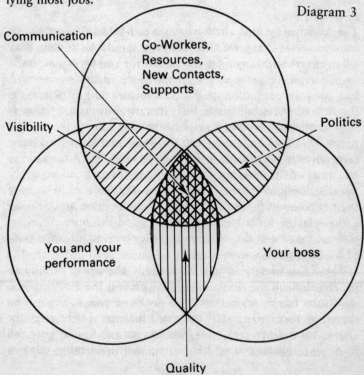

Diagram 3

First, of course, you must pay attention to your own performance in the job; second, you must take stock of your relationship with your boss; and third, you must consider the other people you work with, both in and outside your organization. We will deal with each of these points in more detail in subsequent chapters.

Diagram 3 illustrates four other factors (shaded areas) which can too easily be overlooked. We will examine these now because they must be understood by anyone with career ambitions since they affect almost every aspect of a strategy for advancement. Women, particularly, who often tend to assume rather naively that their success depends solely upon productivity and good performance at work, need to be aware of these factors and learn how they can operate them to their own best advantage.

Politics

The concise Oxford dictionary defines a *politic* person as someone who is sagacious or prudent. A Canadian dictionary enlarges on this by saying it means 'wise in looking out for one's own interest'. It's true that the Oxford also provides a second, less attractive definition: *politic* can mean crafty or scheming. But instead of latching on to this latter, negative connotation as they so often do, women should be more mindful of the sensible notion that they have every right to look after their own interests. Possibly because women have always been encouraged to put others first, in particular their husbands and children, self-interest does not come easily to them, whereas men, who have been exposed to the cut and thrust of competition and political games-playing for a long time, understand the rules. Working women are new to the arena and so they need to learn the skills of business politics from scratch.

These skills have become increasingly important as modern organizations have evolved into their present less authoritarian structures. For example, companies are more open to negotiation than they were in the past. This means that you may be given the chance to sit down with your boss or your other colleagues and to deal with them openly and frankly across the table, but you would be foolish to attempt to do this without having a clear picture of your own self-interest.

Such meetings require groundwork. You must learn who the most influential people are and understand something about their likes and dislikes, as well as their styles and habits in decision-making. Using this understanding as a framework, you can set out to achieve your own objective on terms that are acceptable to you.

Take Susan, for instance, who sells air time for a television company. She got wind of the fact that the company was reorganizing some of its assignments. Keen to expand her sales territory and thus earn more commission as well as gain extra responsibility, she went straight to the managing director – the ultimate decision maker in this instance – and proposed that he enlarge her territory to include some of the regions under discussion. She had made out a good case for the merger and he was impressed by her arguments, so, after some thought, he agreed to the proposal. Susan increased her commission by 30 per cent in the following ten months, leaving her less politically astute colleagues way behind. Susan did nothing wrong; she was just quicker off the mark than anyone else and shrewd enough to see she would get nowhere unless she prepared a first-class plan and took it straight to the top person.

Communication

Again we resort to the dictionary which says that communication is 'the act of imparting information . . . a connection between places'. Both definitions are relevant for the woman wishing to move up. Communication is one of the connections between where she is and where she wants to go. Further, nobody is going to find her in the haystack of modern corporate life unless she tells them where to look.

As the old saying goes, actions speak louder than words but, in the complex politics of the business world, we can't emphasize enough the importance of making sure that your actions are fully understood. This means more than just saying clearly what you want to say. You may be conveying quite accurate information in the messages you put out but if your body language or general behaviour contradicts that content, you shouldn't really be surprised if the receiver of your message misunderstands what you are saying.

In his recent book *Silent Messages*, Albert Mehrabian writes: 'Our silent messages may contradict or reinforce what we say in words; in either event, they are more potent in communications than the words we speak.'

Take Andrea who works as a book-keeper in a non-profit making organization. She wants to increase her salary and would like to become the office manager. When she approached her boss and suggested herself for the new position, and an increase in salary to match the extra responsibility, her boss responded with some amazement: 'Although I know you work well, each time I ask you to take on more responsibility – like chasing up members who haven't paid their subscriptions – you shy away from the situation.'

Andrea didn't realize that she was giving out these confusing messages. She hadn't wanted to appear pushy, but now she realizes that if she wants more responsibility, she must make it crystal clear that she can handle it and is eager to take it on.

Quality

Back to the dictionary once more and here the definitions abound. Quality is a 'degree of excellence . . . a faculty, skill, accomplishment, characteristic, trait, mental or moral attribute'. Quality is probably a woman's major asset in the workplace. It can also be a handicap because very often women over-achieve and find it impossible to settle for the less than perfect; yet there are times in a working life when a mediocre performance is all that is required. Knowing when not to be a perfectionist is a matter of confidence and experience which teaches you how to sort out priorities.

Take the example of Jacqueline and Peter who are both senior managers in a national charity. Recently the topic of computerization came up and each of them was asked by the director to bring to a group management meeting some preliminary thoughts about improving the systems throughout the organization. Jacqueline spent two whole days researching this area and produced a ten-page report. Peter went back to his office, consulted one or two people, spent an hour reading some appropriate material and followed this up with another one-hour discussion to get a grasp of the key issues. He then considered himself prepared for the meeting. Peter did the right thing; Jacqueline, on the other hand, spent too much of her valuable time on something that was less important than other work she could have been doing.

Visibility

To be visible, says the dictionary, means 'can be seen by the eye . . . can be perceived and ascertained . . . to be apparent, open'. Visibility in an organization is obviously important because unless others are made aware of the quality of your work, and see how well you fit in with the organization, you aren't going to get very far.

Joanna is a superbly efficient administrator who has completely reorganized a regional office of the large multinational company for which she works. She would now like to move to head office and take over one of the larger foreign departments. The trouble is that she has accomplished her task so smoothly and quietly that everyone takes her for granted and assumes she is content to remain where she is. She has not made enough noise about herself and her achievements. Like many women she is no good at blowing her own trumpet but if she's going to get ahead she has got to make sure that people appreciate her worth.

A sense of timing

What has been left out of Diagram 3 is a sense of timing, but it's a skill which is every bit as important to the woman who wants to get ahead as it is to the actor. For example, it seldom occurs that the promotion you want comes through at exactly the right time. A working life is as full of surprises as any other part of existence, so you should be ready to seize opportunities when they appear. Equally, you must be prepared to be patient if waiting proves necessary.

Everyone who sets out to succeed is bound to encounter some obstacles on the road to advancement. They may be organizational or personal but, whatever the case, their successful negotiation often depends on a good sense of timing.

If you're lucky enough to be part of an organization that's going through a period of rapid growth or dynamic change, then you will have plenty of opportunities to make your own mark. New challenges are there for the asking so make certain that you're ready to take them up by being in the right place at the right time.

If, on the other hand, your organization is experiencing tough times, you may have a chance to show your leadership skills. For instance, an ability to cut corners is invaluable at times like this. Be the one who develops an effective cost-saving plan.

A good sense of timing also plays a crucial role in personal relations at work – never to be forgotten in any career plan. Timing determines what you say and when, whether it is appropriate to come on strong or keep a low profile. Consider the sad story of Karen who lost her best supporter because her sense of timing was ill-judged.

Karen was a hospital social worker. She had been doing well at her job and was respected by her colleagues for her ability to justify her opinions as well as to arouse their enthusiasm. She enjoyed an excellent relationship with the departmental head, her boss. In private their contact was easy-going and friendly. Sometimes she would point out his failings and he would listen to her and take her criticisms to heart. Then one day she made a serious mistake. She criticized him severely in front of other members of the department.

The results were disastrous. Karen lost all credibility because no one in the department, particularly her boss, felt that they could trust her anymore. It took her two years to regain any measure of respect within the group and her promotion, when it came, was not as good as she had hoped. It's a basic lesson in common sense: most people do not want to experience what Karen's boss experienced in front of others.

The moral of this story is that there are times when it's crucial to keep a low profile, remaining in the background rather than attemtping to move into the limelight.

Almost every situation offers you the opportunity to make a

mistake, so timing is crucial at every level of advancement and should be kept under constant review. If, for instance, you are ready to seize an opportunity in your company but sense that the time may not be right for the company itself, don't push it. It is better to strike when the iron has had time to get hot than when it's lukewarm.

Planning – the essential elements

In the last chapter we talked about the importance of goal-setting – both long- and short-term – and of implementing specific strategies for making these goals come true. In this chapter we have considered five other general factors that will influence your advancement.

Now it's time to incorporate this information in a comprehensive plan for your future. The following three chapters will cover the three essential aspects of any career plan. Briefly, they are:

Strategy 1: Dancing as fast as you can:
Doing the best job possible where you are now

Strategy 2: Ready, steady . . .
How to prepare to leave your present position

Strategy 3: Go!
How to get there from here

Before we discuss these strategies in detail, and bearing in mind what you have already learnt about career planning from reading so far, we suggest you fill in the following worksheet before going on to chapter 3.

WORKSHEET 2

Assessing Possibilities

Fill in the worksheet carefully, remembering to be as specific and realistic as possible in defining possibilities, obstacles and solutions. Also note for yourself the dates by which you want to accomplish solutions. Don't feel restricted by the numbers we have put.

OPPORTUNITIES FOR ADVANCEMENT	OBSTACLES	SOLUTIONS	DATE
Within your industry			
1.			
2.			
3.			
Within your company			
1.			
2.			
3.			
With your boss			
1.			
2.			
3.			

Summary

* Don't be afraid to dream
* Take a good look at your current environment and assess the possibilities in it
* Develop your understanding of what is meant by politics, quality, communication and visibility
* Cultivate a good sense of timing

Dancing as Fast as You Can:
Doing the Best Job Possible
Where You Are Now

Whether you have been in your present position for a few years or you have been recently promoted, transferred or hired, you will find that the steps we outline in this chapter are ones you can't afford to miss out if you want to make an effective career plan. At this point in your career your main aim is to ensure that you are competent in the work required from you in your current position. Start by asking yourself whether you are getting the most from your job? Have you maximized its potential? If you haven't, you are short-changing yourself as well as your company.

The main aim of this chapter is to show you ways of developing your present skills in order to become a more competent, useful person in the workplace, but consider just for a moment the position from your company's point of view. Have you appreciated that you represent a sizeable investment to your company? Consider the time and money that was spent on hiring you: advertising the job, sometimes senior executives interviewing you, internal meetings and so on. Then there is the continuing effort required to manage not only you but also the support services you require to do your job. Your company bears the expense of providing you with the tools you need to do your job, be they a typewriter, calculator, computer, company car or travel allowance. Your company does, however, have another responsibility, and that is directly towards you; it should be making you feel that you have the opportunity to grow.

Developing a positive attitude to your work

In the best of all possible worlds, employer and employees would work together harmoniously and to each other's mutual benefit. Unfortunately, there are many surveys to suggest that in the real world of work the situation is far from ideal. Far too large a proportion of the working population is not deriving job satisfaction. There are a few progressive companies which have made substantial investments in recent years to create new ways of working at particular tasks, and they have devised productivity and incentive schemes to sustain job satisfaction.

But if it happens that you are one of the unlucky ones who is dissatisfied with her present job, do try to conceal your feelings at work. A positive attitude is crucial to moving up, so use your dissatisfaction to plan for advancement; otherwise you will reach a plateau of job performance which is bad for your morale and could damage your future.

Remember what happened to Janice? Her negative and self-defeating attitudes finally made it impossible for her to continue in a job where she had been given the chance to prove herself. You can retain your individuality without also being the loudest or the most outrageous person in the office. Obviously you don't want to turn into a mealy-mouthed yes-woman, but being a rebel for the sake of it, and getting too much of a reputation for non-conformity, is not going to stand you in good stead either.

Work relationships are very important. Without turning into a creep, it is worth your while to make an effort to understand your boss's personal working style and preferences. In other words try to be cooperative rather than negative and, if you can, develop a dialogue so that he or she realizes you are willing and able to take on more responsibility. Other relationships are equally important: learning to be a good team player and working well with all sorts of people at different levels will prepare you for taking on more senior managerial work.

If you are offered opportunities to attend conferences or other more social events connected with your company's business, do take them. These occasions give you a chance to make new contacts, exchange information and consolidate your working relationships in easier, less formal surroundings. But it's unwise to relax completely. We are not saying that you should never mix business with pleasure, but for women especially the borderline between ordinary socializing and closer relationships is fraught with perils. We shall be saying more about this in chapter 6.

Acquiring skills related to your present position

Although it helps to be popular with your colleagues, a pleasing personality is not enough to qualify you for success. Indeed people who are too anxious to please may not be doing themselves a favour. Before you can even start to think of moving up in an organization you must be on top of the job you are currently doing. This means having all the necessary skills at your fingertips so that you project yourself as a professional and capable person.

Lorraine is an administrative assistant to a wholesale dress manufacturer. She has studied for a fashion diploma at night school and aims to become a production manager. At the moment she is being trained to read computer reports in order to help her boss forecast the purchase of raw materials. The significant skill for Lorraine is that she is learning how to analyse data and relate the results to future decision making and scheduling. Her keen interest in this activity is helping her perform well in her present job and her acquired competence will stand her in good stead when she applies for more advanced training.

When you get to the point of feeling totally at ease in your job, and knowledgeable enough to be able to handle any setbacks or crises, then you can start looking for work-related activities round the office; for example, you might want to volunteer to serve on a staff committee or become involved with some aspect of public relations which brings you into closer contact with the company's clients. It's all part of getting connected.

Getting connected and networking

This is another important aspect of working life which women, particularly, sometimes tend to overlook. Doing your job well is obviously essential if you want to get on but don't imagine that you will be rewarded on performance alone. If you can show that you are alert to what is going on around you and that you are interested in your company's wider objectives, not just what you can get out of it for yourself, you are much more likely to become a candidate for promotion. Getting connected is a vital part of getting ahead.

Never despise the office grapevine. Information travels fast along it and it's never a waste of time to take note of what you hear. Keep in touch with people who may not be high in the hierarchy but who do have an uncanny way of knowing what's going on. This tactic can be especially useful for women who work in areas dominated by the masculine ethos and style of management – engineering, the law, finance, to give a few examples. Such women, particularly if they are few in numbers, often find that they are the last to hear about important changes. Sometimes they get the company news at just about the same time as a public announcement. Even when they think they have been present at a meeting finalizing some important decision, they discover later that it's all been reversed during a casual conversation in the men's room.

When feminist academics first started to examine the dynamics of success with a view to discovering the magic formula which, up till then, seemed largely to have escaped women, one of the first things they learned by studying successful men was just how significant a role the so-called 'old boys network' played in high-level achievement. Networking, the deliberate cultivation of useful contacts both in and outside the office, has become an important part of women's working life in recent years. The old adage 'it's not what you know but who you know' still rings true for many a success story.

It's often difficult for women to break into a male network. Many of these circles aren't even very congenial to women – the exclusive man's club or the hearty locker room are not natural female habitats – but nowadays there are women's network groups, enough to cater for most interests.

That is how most of the flourishing ones in our list were started. A few women feeling isolated and unsupported in their work getting together and holding informal meetings where they could discuss issues and share problems. Gradually these meetings turned into other events like short seminars, evening lectures, talks from senior women in other industries, careers days and so on.

Look at our resource list at the end of the book and if you can't find one locally that relates to your own industry, you could either set up a branch of a national one in your area or create a new one inside your own company.

All these groups are friendly and welcoming. Their membership subscriptions are deliberately kept as low as possible and they usually produce a newsletter so that out-of-town members can keep in touch with what's going on – among themselves as well as in their industry. You don't have to go through awful initiation rites or swear to any ideology to prove your eligibility.

Managing your boss

A good boss is hard to find. If you have one, she or he should be highly valued. Not only are bosses privy to important company information which they can share with you; they are also your link with top management.

Don't, however, expect too much of your boss. There's no reason why your boss should understand your point of view, know your work history, or sympathize with your desires or your expectations unless you make a point of communicating these matters, at the appropriate moment, of course.

What follows is a list of suggestions for mounting a successful communications campaign with your boss.

1. Be approachable. If your boss asks you for your opinion respond positively with ideas or alternatives. Saying you haven't got a clue means that you won't be asked again and you have

thus cut yourself off from a potentially useful connection and source of information. Similarly, don't be afraid to volunteer suggestions, before you're asked, if you think you have something useful to say.

2. Should differences occur between you and your boss or your colleagues, be the one to clear the air. This will earn you the reputation of being a diplomat. It will also help you to assess how good your boss is at communicating, an important consideration when it comes to discussing promotions, benefits and other matters of interest to you.

3. Always try to depersonalize any differences of opinion that may occur between you and your boss, or your colleagues. Try and keep your comments on difficult situations to a cool, factual discussion of the issues involved. Sometimes it can be very difficult to keep your feelings in check, particularly if you suspect someone is misrepresenting you, but emotional reactions in a business setting are usually counterproductive.

4. Find out what kind of assistance your boss most needs and appreciates so that you can effectively lighten the workload.

5. Seek support from your boss when the need arises and don't wait to do so until the last moment. For instance, if you can see a problem arising in the near future to do with a sick child, or some other kind of private crisis, discuss ways of solving it beforehand so that your boss is not left in the lurch.

6. Indicate your commitment to your job by making it clear that you are available for special projects and overtime. On the other hand, don't allow yourself to be turned into the office dogsbody who is at everyone's beck and call. You will only end up feeling ill-used and resentful.

7. Make sure that you get regular performance appraisals. Some companies do this as a matter of course but if you are in one where it has not yet become an established procedure, insist, tactfully, that you do want such appraisals so that you can monitor your progress.

8. Be specific about your consistent desire to be informed as well as to advance, and don't be shy about commenting on new

developments within the organization. It shows that you're keen and interested.

All these recommendations require a certain self-confidence and maturity to be able to put them into practice. If you find it hard to say no, difficult to put forward your point of view, or intimidating to initiate a discussion when it is your interests that are at stake, then you should definitely consider investing in an assertiveness training course.

This training varies in form and content: some courses are run once a week over several weeks with home exercises in between; others are structured more intensively to last one or two days, possibly with a follow-up day several months later. Whatever way they are devised, the aim is the same: to help you overcome personal inhibitions about communicating what you want which may make you either timid and diffident, or excessively pushy and demanding. Many of the exercises are based on learning new behavioural responses in a variety of situations, but they won't have a long-term effect unless you are prepared to change your attitude as well. When you see what wonders a firm, controlled manner can produce, even in little incidents like getting courteous treatment from a recalcitrant shop assistant, you will think it well worth while.

All the names on our resource list are recommended consultants and trainers who have made a speciality of this particular training. They run courses both for companies and individuals; for the latter, who are paying out of their own pocket, they are usually very reasonably priced.

If you have to negotiate a special agreement where you may have ambivalent feelings about the outcome, try and keep them to yourself. A specific example is the case of Marjorie who is a chartered surveyor in a medium-sized firm. She has been there for eight years and has certainly proved her worth. She is liked and respected by her colleagues, and James, the senior partner in the firm, thinks highly of her. She recently became pregnant but she plans to return to work as soon as she feels happy about leaving the day-time nanny in charge of the baby. She had a long talk with James and confidently told him she would be returning.

Unfortunately, she also let slip that her husband and parents on both sides were pressuring her to stay at home.

James told Marjorie how much he valued her contribution; at the same time this little confession worries him. He fears her family may persuade her not to return but, even if she does, he thinks she may have less energy for the job if she is torn by the conflicting demands they make on her. Now, however well Marjorie performs at work when she gets back from her maternity leave, James is always going to have this nagging doubt about her ability to stick it out. Will it be worth offering her a partnership?

Helen, who is a solicitor in a large city practice, decided to wait until she had been offered a partnership before she started a family. After two years she was well established with a faithful clientele, so when she announced her pregnancy she had no problem in negotiating her maternity leave. She organized her case load so that urgent matters were handled by colleagues in her absence, and all her clients were reassured by her calm, organized way of handling the situation. When the baby was three months old, she came back on a part-time basis and at six months she was fully back in the saddle.

Combining children with a career is not easy. Women who are starting on this track are well advised to conceal any private worries they may have about their ability to cope. Apart from undermining their own determination it is not going to help their case with their employer. A few companies do now organize excellent career-break schemes for their employees – the clearing banks and some of the big companies like Marconi and Ferranti are pioneers in this area – but most organizations still feel apprehensive. Don't give them any extra cause for concern.

If a new boss takes over, particularly someone who is new to the organization or comes from another area, set the tone early by putting out signals about your interest in getting on. But do be subtle about it. Don't just walk in and say, 'I want to get ahead' because that's threatening and therefore off-putting. Do discuss some of your previous work history, and, where possible, make it clear that you took the initiative to get where you are. Don't brag, be honest; but have no hesitation in pointing out the positive aspects of your working relationships: this will help convey the message that you're a good team player.

One word of warning: as with everything else in life, when your objective is to move up through your organization, timing is crucial. You should only make a point of informing your boss about your desire to advance when you are certain that your present position is under control. It's all too easy to fall into the trap of spreading yourself too thin in your current job because you are over-anxious to prove yourself in other areas of work.

Belinda's story illustrates the dangers of allowing yourself to be so carried away by ambition that your tactical judgement goes out of the window. In her case it resulted in losing the promotion for which she was supremely well qualified.

Belinda had been appointed director of in-service nurse education for the District Health Authority. She appeared very committed to her job and she was considered by her superiors to be a success in it. After a couple of years she began to play around with the idea of going into the private sector, either by setting up her own nursing agency or by working for one of the private hospital groups. At several informal gatherings with her colleagues she let it slip that she was thinking of change. She left little doubt that she would eventually make the move, and most of her colleagues felt that it was just a matter of time.

Meanwhile, her immediate boss, the director of nurse education, was promoted and Belinda was an obvious successor with her good qualifications and track record. Based on her past performance, it seemed inevitable that she would be considered as a serious candidate, so she presented her application with confidence.

Unfortunately, she did not even make the short list. At Belinda's request for an explanation, the select committee revealed that her declaration of intent to leave the National Health Service had made them uneasy about her long-term commitment. She was surprised to learn that these concerns were included in their evaluation, but it taught her an important lesson. Until your plans for an alternative job are finalized, don't broadcast them through the organization for which you currently work.

Becoming a team player

Generally speaking, when you begin to work you will be mainly concerned with mastering the major tasks of your job as best you can. You will be focusing your energies on getting along with your superiors and your colleagues on a day-to-day basis. But as you advance in your career, you will be asked to take more responsibility and become involved with specific projects, either as a participant or a leader. Many of these tasks require teamwork.

If you are a loner by habit, you must prevent the antisocial side of your nature from taking over. Otherwise you won't advance: a company can only cope with a few soloists and these usually appear at a later stage. As in an orchestra, there is always a place in business for soloists to prove their skills, but unless you can all play together on cue, you cannot function effectively. An organization thrives because of the combined efforts of all its members. Hence the team.

A woman benefits from being a member of a team because she has other supporters who may advance along with her or even be in a position to promote her. In many ways, it's like having an in-house network; a good team supports each of its members through the various problems they may encounter.

Evelyn has been selling computers for a well-known international company for some years. The only woman in her team, she regularly beats targets and earns a hefty monthly commission. But whatever the rivalries to outdo each other, the team remains solid. 'It's a tremendous team,' she says, 'and great fun to work with because we all care equally, and if one of us is in trouble you can always go and cry on someone's shoulder.' Although she often has to contend with difficult clients who try to proposition her as a condition of the sale, Evelyn has never experienced any sexual harassment from her own team. 'I don't believe they actually see me as a woman. We are quite literally like the best sort of brothers.' Evelyn has achieved acceptance and respect from her colleagues because she works on equal terms and doesn't try to use her sex to take unfair advantage.

Deborah is an insurance company executive and she too has

learnt to work in a team. Her strongest assets are her abilities to make decisions and take innovative risks. Her male colleagues find that she fits in well on new projects and they always ask her to participate. Deborah believes that the more women become involved in teamwork the quicker discrimination will disappear because men will appreciate their professionalism and their capacity to manage.

In our experience, the women who most enjoy their work and are getting to the top the fastest are those who have secured a firm position in their informal working environment. Because they have become good team players, their actions are no longer scrutinized, nor are they victimized for the occasional mistakes they make. As a result they are able to stay in touch and on top of things.

The following tips should help you to become an effective team member:

1. Whenever you are working on a solution to a problem, consider the implications of your behaviour for other people in the organization. Try to take the different personalities and skills of your colleagues into consideration before you act.

2. Make sure that your team is not too big (twelve people or less). Otherwise it can become unwieldy, and besides, the larger the group, the more difficult it will be for you to make a visible contribution.

3. Volunteer to work on those projects, committees and task forces which address issues pertinent to your own work.

4. Choose groups of people who will respect your contribution to the team but who will also give you some autonomy to be innovative, as well as to perform at your own pace and in your own style. Respect your fellow team members' desire for the same things.

5. Make sure that the project you are working on has been given serious backing in the organization and that senior management and the leader of your team are committed to seeing it through to a successful achievement.

6. Try to establish exactly how much time your team

participation will require because this will enable you to meet the team's objectives while allowing you to get on with your other work.

Finally, there are two fundamental questions you should always ask before embarking on a new project, so that you can gauge whether your presence will be productive, or, indeed, is even necessary.

1. *Is a team essential to this task?*
Not all tasks require a team because one person may have all the skills necessary for seeing the project through from start to finish. If, however, there is a need for a team, assess the skills required and then look at who is available. If you have a hand in composing the team try to achieve an effective combination of the various skills and personalities. This matters because you now have to take very seriously the following question in all its ramifications.

2. *How will the team operate?*
Consider all these points:

i. What impact will the current policies and procedures of your organization have on the team?

ii. Do you and your fellow team members share a common perception of the goals in view?

iii. Do you understand the way in which the team is expected to accomplish work, make decisions and communicate, both internally and externally?

iv. Can the team develop external relationships with customers, government, other divisions or organizations? If so, who should handle those relationships, and how?

v. How will you, as a group, handle conflict and chart your progress?

If you don't know the answers to the above questions, you should at least be thinking about them, and, if necessary, raise them with other members of the team. In the same way that you, as an individual, need to set personal goals and plan strategies for achieving them, so does a team. This is called team building.

Developing your skills as a team leader – becoming a team builder

Taking a leadership position in any organization can be exciting as well as exhausting. On certain projects you will welcome the chance to be in a leadership position. On others you may want to take a back seat. Taking a positive view, most projects offer good exposure and, by improving your visibility, they can serve to broaden your contacts within your organization. Furthermore, although they usually involve extra effort, they are also limited to a specific endpoint and duration of time.

Marilyn works for a local authority as a recreation manager. Recently she decided that she wanted to improve certain recreational facilities for the disabled so she set up a working party with representatives from all the relevant departments within the borough – health, community and social services, finance and others. Realizing that each member of the working party had their own valid point of view, Marilyn knew that she must, from the outset, create a clear focus for the group's performance. Her first step, therefore, was to draft a mandate which she took for approval to her senior management group, thus winning their full support for the project from the beginning. This also achieved her objective of clarifying goals and aims for the working party so that it didn't waste any time in discussing its purpose and direction before getting down to the real task of improving facilities. The whole experience proved satisfying and productive and the new facilities have been successfully introduced.

Whether you become a team leader by initiating a project yourself, or because you have been appointed to carry out someone else's idea, the following tips should help you to stay on course.

1. Clarify your team mandate before you get the team together.

2. Try to obtain a clear review in writing of how the project was developed. This should include:

   i. Background details

   ii. Information on the real sponsors who pioneered these developments within the organization

iii. The scope of the project in terms of the extent of research required, the time allocated and the commitment of company resources

iv. The limitations of the project. For instance, is the group to be just an advisory one that makes recommendations, or will it have responsibility for the implementation of its conclusions?

3. Prepare an exhaustive list of the points of view to be examined and the tasks inherent in the team's work, and consult with the relevant people before you make a decision about who should be on the team.

4. Determine what skills are essential to the project and obtain a high level of expertise in these areas.

5. Analyse team performance regularly, and always discuss any changes in circumstances, new goals that may arise and areas of possible improvement.

6. Develop options and action plans for improvement.

7. Record and evaluate team performance.

Planning a personal support system

Once you recognize that your career orientation has shifted from a short-term to a long-term perspective you will have to start thinking more seriously about the balance between your personal and working life. To help you stretch your plan beyond a year, it's important to begin thinking about managing your personal life in such a way that, without sacrificing the pleasures it gives you, it becomes more complementary to your career. One of the first areas to look at is your current support system, and these are the kind of questions you should be asking yourself.

Are you in a position to devote longer hours to your job should a worthwhile opportunity occur? Does your partner support you in your career ambitions? As a single woman, do you have a circle of friends you know you can call on if you are feeling troubled or overstretched? If you have children, and especially if you are a single parent, can your current childcare arrangements sustain a heavier work load? Do you have a reliable fail-safe if there is a family emergency, like a child falling sick? Is your partner cooperative about child care? Are you spending so much time on domestic work when you get home that you are chronically exhausted?

In chapter 4 we deal in more depth with personal support systems and in chapter 6 we look at ways of managing stress. Women sometimes neglect to build up support for themselves at the cost of their health and happiness. It is very important not to fall into the Superwoman trap of doing so much that you drive yourself into the ground. Single women are just as vulnerable as women with families, not least because everyone assumes that they can perfectly well look after themselves. And so they can, but there are pitfalls for them as well.

Take Frances who has always lived on her own and is very particular about her flat and the nice things she has acquired over the years. Her job in a travel agency takes her abroad several times a year. Initially, when asking a friend to water her plants and generally keep an eye on things for her during her absence, she would be very fussy and ultra critical if that person hadn't followed her instructions to the letter. Instead of being appreciative, she got upset, and consequently was always changing her caretakers. The final blow came when even her best friend could stand the criticism no longer and refused to help. At last Frances got the message that building an effective support system involves nurturing the people who help you, remembering to say thank you, overlooking any minor lapses and, whenever possible, offering reciprocal services. No one wants to be left pages of instructions and rewarded with criticism, especially if you don't even return favours.

Learning how to travel alone

At this stage in your career you may not be part of the company jet set, but once you reach a certain level in management it is more than likely that you will be asked to travel. Now is the time to start preparing yourself psychologically, intellectually and physically for travelling on your own.

Women often feel nervous about business travelling. The concerns they voice seem to centre on the fear of being alone in strange places and unease about being separated from their partner or family, quite as much as coping with all the obvious problems which arise from a disrupted routine. It's true that a single woman on her own is still an object of undue interest in some countries, particularly where there are still very traditional conventions about women's social behaviour, but there are ways of warding off unwanted attention. For example, if you have to wait in a public place to keep an appointment, then *look* occupied. Always keep a book or magazine handy.

Think of it like this: if your organization has enough faith in you to send you off on a business trip, then you surely have enough confidence in yourself to cope. Here are some useful tips from other travellers, and as you become more experienced yourself you will be able to add to the list.

1. Get a good travel agent. Even so, never trust anyone but yourself. Reconfirm all flights, hotel reservations and any other arrangements you have made.

2. Get organized. This means making certain your passport is up to date, you have any necessary visas and inoculations, and that your credit cards are valid. Keep a pocket calculator (for currency transactions), appropriate phrasebook and city maps in your handbag. Don't forget your business cards and always carry loose change for tips.

3. Know your itinerary ahead of time. For overseas trips, confirm appointments before you leave, and again on arrival.

4. Pack clothes *suitable* for your appointments. You may be travelling abroad but this is not a holiday. Even if you prefer to travel in comfortable casual clothes, be sure to walk off the plane in a working outfit so that you are ready for your first appointment.

5. Travel as light as possible, preferably hand luggage only for short trips so that you don't have to hang around waiting for suitcases to be unloaded. When packing, observe the rules of common sense. For instance, have a basic colour theme so that you can keep your accessories to a minimum; use an unbreakable set of

essential cosmetics; if you do have more than one piece of luggage, keep a spare set of underclothes, blouse, skirt, etc. just in case your luggage goes missing.

6. Other essential travel items should include:
> travel alarm clock
> folding bag for unexpected extra luggage
> travelling iron and hair dryer with appropriate electric current for your destination
> sewing kit
> any medicine you may need, such as aspirin or something for an upset stomach

7. Don't eat or drink too much in transit – it increases jet lag.

8. When carrying cash, keep it in two places: you can often take advantage of hotel safety deposit boxes. And keep your jewellery to a minimum; you won't need a lot of it.

9. If you feel uncomfortable eating alone in a public dining room, order room service and enjoy the television or a good book.

10. Pay your way if you are in a group of people – your share of a meal or a round of drinks – except, of course, if you are being entertained by a client.

Paying attention to the company image

Presenting a polished, self-confident image of yourself acts as a powerful tool of communication and helps you to get a message across. While you should take some care to adjust your manner of speaking and your vocabulary to the different audiences you're trying to reach, don't compromise your own individuality in so doing. The same applies to the way you dress. Of course it's important to dress in a style which is appropriate to your company image, but don't allow yourself to be taken over by the pin-striped brigade, male or female. Even in those professions like the law, for instance, where women are obliged to dress in sober greys and blacks, they can still assert their personal style by small touches like wearing pretty shirts, bright scarves and so on.

If you feel unsure about your fashion style then it could be worthwhile having a session with a colour consultant and/or a wardrobe 'weeder' who will go right through all your clothes and advise you what to keep and what to throw out, and what to get where that is up to date and appropriate to your working life. The money you spend on her fee will, in the long run, be a saving as she will prevent you from making expensive mistakes in the future. There is also a useful guideline chapter on dressing in *The Working Woman's Handbook* (see Further Reading). Ignoring your personal appearance, or expecting people to take you as you are – unkempt hair, over made-up or badly – is unwise, especially as you progress in a company which will be assessing you on your social as well as your professional skills. First impressions are lasting. If you make a bad one, you'll waste a lot of valuable time trying to counteract it.

Dress is an obvious expression of a corporate image but there are other more subtle ones and each organization has its own culture relating to professional image and style. Most companies will expect their employees to do a certain amount of socializing, both internally and externally with clients. Some companies even expect their employees to take part in a number of voluntary activities. Styles of speech also vary; bad language is commonplace in some companies, taboo in others.

Most organizations wait a while before they make the major investment in someone which a promotion represents. The kinds of social tests mentioned above are combined with performance reviews to provide employers with the information they need to make a sound assessment of their potential investment. If you're on the receiving end of this testing process, it's easy to underestimate its significance and to become impatient with it. Don't! Just accept that it's inevitable and that you are going to make the most of it. If you are nervous about yourself it might be worth investing in a self-presentation course (see Resources).

Politics, communication, quality, visibility and timing

As we said in chapter 2, these five factors play a part in every stage of your career. Take a look at them now in the context of the points made in this chapter.

The importance of politics in your working life should now be clear to you. It is implicit in many of the tips we have presented here: getting connected, learning to manage your boss, making it known that you want to get on, paying attention to the corporate image. Nowhere is it more important than in your contribution to teamwork and leadership. By working on teams you can acquire an understanding – both formal and informal – of the group dynamics of your company as well as the personalities of key co-workers. You can also pick up the buzz words, the images that are respected, the leadership styles that are most accepted, the sort of performance in group tasks that is most valued. All of this will be enormously useful to you as you climb the corporate ladder.

Communication affects every exchange you have with your co-workers. Unfortunately, women tend to be evaluated twice – on their femininity as well as their competence. Be the sort of woman you want to be – dress and talk in the way that is natural to you without either overtly trading on your sex or trying to deny it. And don't let your body language or your actions say something that you don't want to say. For instance, a friend of Ruth's once told her that her boss had told her to clean up her language if she wanted to get ahead in his organization. She hadn't noticed that she was the only employee who used bad language.

A loud voice, mannerisms, a confrontational style or teasing don't work well for women in work circles. They shouldn't for men either, but because the culture of the workplace is still male-dominated and imbued with macho attitudes they can get away with more or worse. It's unfair but it's a fact of life. All the same, don't be scared into becoming unduly stiff or formal in your working relationships. When presenting material at meetings, for instance, be concise and well organized while retaining a relaxed manner; don't read your reports as if they were sermons.

As far as quality is concerned, are you delivering the best work possible in all areas of your job? Sometimes 'the best work possible' means less than perfect; you will have to decide which tasks require time-consuming, in-depth research and which tasks demand only a superficial, quick study. A perceptive boss will understand why you spend a whole week on one task, a few hours on another; in fact, he or she should applaud your judgement in deciding what level of excellence is appropriate to a given job. As in so many ways, working in a team is invaluable here. It allows you to see what sort of quality your colleagues deliver and expect of each other.

Working in a team is also the quickest way to achieve visibility in your organization. Getting connected with a network of colleagues – both in and outside the office – is another effective tool. Finally, making sure that you have regular reviews and appraisals with your boss will keep you in the foreground because it enables you to remind him or her of what you have already accomplished.

We've mentioned the role of timing several times in this chapter – letting your boss know you want to advance, for instance. It's crucial, particularly when you are making demands on your boss or fellow workers.

These factors all interact with each other: political know-how and timing go hand in hand, as do communication and visibility. Don't focus on one at the expense of another.

As you fill in the following worksheet, look at each category and see how many gaps there are in your overall effectiveness. You will probably have more positive answers in some categories than in others. All the categories – your competency, your company, your boss, your peers and your home life – are important, so if your answers reveal weaknesses in one or two areas, work on those, bearing in mind that they all complement each other.

WORKSHEET 3

Where Are You Now?

YOUR COMPETENCY
In order to advance you must be performing competently at your current level. This first group of questions is intended to measure your competency.

1. What are the basic responsibilities of your current position?

2. Are you competent in all of them? If not, how can you improve your performance?

3. Have you received a positive performance appraisal?

4. Can you receive any merits for making an outstanding contribution?

5. Have you documented your contributions in a work file?

6. Are there any skills in your current position which you have not yet acquired that could be useful to you in the futute?

YOU AND YOUR COMPANY
The following questions will help you to evaluate your own visibility within your organization.

1. Are you prepared to volunteer for extra activities. If so, which ones? Are there other possibilities that could be useful to you?

2. How far do you pay your dues in terms of dress, image, jargon?

3. Do you voice your opinions and ideas in meetings?

4. If travel is a possibility in your job, are you prepared for it, mentally and organizationally?

YOU AND YOUR BOSS

Sometimes you may have everything going for you, but your boss is a potential liability. He or she controls your entries and exits in the company. Here are some questions to help you assess whether he or she is doing a good job for you.

1. Are you able to contribute to your company in a way that makes your boss look good?

2. Have you let your boss know that you like changes, particularly ones that lead to new developments?

3. Does your boss give you credit for your achievements?

4. Do you have a good working relationship with your boss? If not, how can you improve it?

YOU AND YOUR HOME LIFE

Think again about the impact of your home life on your ability to work well, especially if you have children.

1. Have you made adequate arrangements for child care and domestic chores to enable you to do your job at work?

2. Do you have a contingency plan in the event of a home emergency?

YOU AND YOUR PEERS

The importance of your relationships with your colleagues cannot be overestimated. After all, they may be on the next selection committee for a plum job or assignment.

1. Do you think your peers see you as a team player?

2. Do you have a mentor?

3. Have you developed a professional network both in and outside the office?

Summary

These are some of the most immediate tasks you should be working on in the here and now.

* Aim to get a good performance appraisal
* Update your job description and arrange to review it with your boss
* Become a team player
* Get involved in the company grapevine
* Start networking
* Become assertive
* Polish up your image

4

Ready, Steady . . .
How to Prepare to Leave
Your Present Position

Since the spate of reforming legislation in the mid-1970s to promote equal pay and equal opportunities, the position of women has definitely improved in several respects. On the work front, although they are currently earning only an average 74 per cent of men's income, they are beginning to do all sorts of jobs which would have been unthinkable only a few years ago. Most women now accept that they will always be working outside the home and they are organizing their careers accordingly. The very fact that you are reading this book testifies to your determination to acquire the necessary skills and understanding for career advancement. So, yes, to paraphrase the Virginia Slims cigarette slogan, we have come some of the way but we've still got a lot of ground to make up.

Women are proving themselves to be quite adept at learning new areas of expertise; for instance, most have learned the value of being a good team player. However, there are some easily identifiable skills which women still lack and which we will discuss in more depth in chapter 5. Women also have some bad habits which they find difficult to break, probably because they are often still operating according to the 'old scripts' which were handed out to them when they were growing up. For example, the desire to please makes it difficult to say 'no' firmly; and the pressure to prove that you can be a perfect wife, mother, lover has a way of spilling over into your working life as well so that you find it almost impossible to delegate. It's a fairly typical phenomenon to see women accepting too much work, assuming too much responsibility and demanding absolute perfection of themselves. Bad habits are made to be broken. Read on and we'll explain how you can do it.

The benefits of delegation

Being unable to delegate means that you haven't really thought what the positive benefits could be for you if you did hand over some of your more mundane jobs. Instructing someone else in the particulars of a task and making sure that they do it properly does cost quite a lot of time and effort at the beginning. But you should remember that the hours you spend training a subordinate to do certain work now will eventually save you a great deal of time. In other words, delegation should be seen as an investment in your own future, so to ignore it is a mistake for any woman drawing up her long-term plans to move up in management.

One of the reasons why women find it hard to delegate is that often they are such determined perfectionists that they are reluctant to ask someone else to do what they consider to be part of their jobs. They are afraid that other people are going to think they aren't capable of handling things themselves. Nothing could be further from the truth.

In her long experience of running courses and workshops for women managers, Ruth has found that one of the most common problems to crop up is time management. And when she analyses why this should be, invariably she finds that the failure to delegate is the root cause of the problem. Wherever you are in management, you must realize that delegation is neither a sign of inadequacy nor of making unreasonable demands on others; it's simply part of your job to be able to organize priorities – and your staff – in such a way that you are enabled to be super effective at your own job. A good manager will delegate whatever routine job he or she can find, just like an efficiently organized working mother shares out the domestic chores among the family and buys in whatever help or services she can afford so that she can make the most of her precious time with her family.

Take the good example of Rosemary, a management consultant who provides a variety of services to her clients. One of these is the development of educational tools for training purposes. In her early years of practice, Rosemary prepared all the materials herself and produced a dossier for teaching manuals along with some very specific guidelines for their preparation. As her work increased, Rosemary hired a research assistant, at first employing her only to research manuals that were still at the development stage. When the researcher had become more familiar with the programmes, Rosemary extended her responsibilities until finally she was preparing drafts of manuals. The researcher became ever more interested and capable, to the point that Rosemary now delegates the entire written material production to her.

Rosemary's initial investment in training the researcher was heavy. She had to brief her carefully and give her clear guidelines for each task, being quite specific about such details as the number of pages she wanted in a manual and the amount of space she wanted devoted to particular subjects. She also had to issue firm deadlines and monitor progress every step of the way.

This may seem like a lot of work – and it is – but Rosemary's investment has really paid off. She now has a first-rate, dependable assistant who appreciates the training and opportunity for growth that she has been given. For her part, Rosemary is delighted to be released to have more time building up the business and maintaining her client contacts.

Delegation, properly done, is neither exploitative nor manipulative. On the contrary, it develops other people as well as assisting you and it is a fundamental managerial skill. People who don't delegate are liable to become snowed under, harassed and passed over.

The first step towards successful delegation is to become more specific in the way you run your working relationships. Define your needs by scheduling objectives and make sure that everyone understands them. Be prepared to allow your subordinates a little time to become accustomed to your style. It's essential to give them input: clarify your standards and the results you expect from each task you give them. Make a point of defining

69

both their individual responsibilities and the scope of their authority. While allowing them autonomy, regularly check with them that they are keeping to guidelines and are not being waylaid.

If you have just been promoted into a new position, you may find that your first attempts at delegation meet with a negative response from your staff. People are often rather defensive with a new boss. They are worrying more about themselves than you, but sometimes it's hard to determine whether the problem is to do with being a boss or being a woman or both. You may never know and it really doesn't matter. The only way to solve it is by doing the best job that you can and convincing your staff that you deserve their respect. Always be polite and considerate but don't delegate tasks as if you were asking a favour. You are, after all, the boss.

The better you become at delegating, the more at ease you will feel in your managerial role. And as you gain confidence so too will your staff become more supportive and positive towards you. To be able to manage a group of people with varying specialist skills means that you will produce the end results that you, as manager, have been employed to achieve, almost as if you yourself were in possession of all those specialized skills.

Another art which many women find hard to learn, and which dovetails closely with delegation, is being able to say 'no' effectively and without causing offence. For instance, it's not sensible to take on any and every assignment which comes your way. Obviously some dull projects can't be avoided but you should make a point of assessing everything that is offered to you in terms not just of what you can do for it but what it can do for you. As much as possible you should be looking for opportunities to increase your knowledge, enhance your visibility and chalk up brownie points with someone who counts. Whatever the task, once you have taken it on, it is your responsibility to monitor its progress and make sure that it is completed on time but remember, that doesn't mean you have to do it all yourself. The skill lies in deciding what can be delegated and to whom. It's no good delegating to someone you want to be kind to but who isn't actually up to the job, at least not yet.

Grooming your successor

Women who are ambitious to move on should always train up a successor so that they don't get caught in the trap of their own success. So often it happens that a woman who performs outstandingly well in her job finds it hard to be promoted.

To explain this disconcerting paradox, consider the story of Lynne, a high-level credit manager in a bank. After ten years with the bank, during which time she has done her banking exams and worked her way up to a job in head office, she is now handling some major accounts. She has been in this position for four years and has performed well for which she has received some handsome bonuses. Moreover, her colleagues have recommended promotion for her since she has worked longer in that department than anyone else.

Lynne too has made a point of indicating her interest in moving up. She always goes to the right meetings and communicates regularly with her boss but over the last six months she has become uneasy. Two new positions opened up in the bank. Lynne applied for them both but to her chagrin was passed over on each occasion.

Understandably furious, she discussed the problem with her manager, who told her that the timing was not good for her department. Some weeks later, still angry, Lynne requested a performance appraisal. Again she came through with flying colours, so this time she decided to discuss the situation with the chief executive.

Where had she gone wrong? she demanded. An in-depth review and discussion at this level revealed that her performance left nothing to be desired. Indeed, she had maintained the highest standards of anyone in her department. All the procedures and accounts were at her fingertips. The problem was that she had never shared her knowledge or trained anyone else to perform some of the tasks she knew so well. She had, in effect, made herself indispensable.

The chief executive gave her some invaluable advice: he told her to become more aware of the people working immediately below her. He arranged for her to speak to a particular manager, the intention being to discover who would be next in line for a position such as hers. The message came through loud and clear: if Lynne wanted to advance, she should be grooming a suitable successor.

Herein lies an important lesson for many women who, in their drive to excel, produce high-quality results and in so doing become workaholics. Many women have two jobs anyway and yet they are quite prepared to expand their responsibilities so that they become overloaded. It has something to do with gaining experience but also we suspect – men as well as women – that it may also be to compensate for feelings of insecurity.

It's important to understand that once a territory, an area of work, has been thoroughly mastered, it should be renegotiated. If you persist in hanging on to what you have, and simultaneously assume responsibility for more and more, you run the risk of becoming indispensable where you are and thus unpromotable.

On one level it's easy to sympathize with the many women who feel, not without justification, that their company would prefer to have a man in their place. This makes them untrusting. They don't like the idea of someone taking over their tasks because they fear they will be ousted from the position they have fought so hard to reach. It's a vicious circle: they avoid training others to take their place because they are frightened they won't be promoted, yet, unless they make a serious stab at finding a good replacement for themselves, the company will be reluctant to move them up because it doesn't want a great gaping hole in the corporate fabric.

If you have already begun to delegate tasks, then you are on your way to grooming an ultimate replacement for yourself. Here are some useful tips:

1. Many routine jobs can be delegated. Monitor the performance of your subordinates to see who works best at specific tasks and shows the greatest interest in them.

2. Create a keen learner by developing a strong supervisory interest in, or relationship with, the person who shows the greatest interest in your area and in advancing there.

3. Encourage such a person to join you in some of your tasks, first as an observer.

4. If they are interested in what they see, start to teach them in a step-by-step fashion how to perform the tasks. Don't forget to give them immediate constructive feedback on each advance that they make.

5. Raise your expectations for the next task and see how they fare.

6. Discuss their anxieties or problems along the way.

As you can see, grooming a replacement is just a specialized form of delegating tasks. Not only will it free you eventually from some of your present workload, but it will also give you the satisfaction of having passed on some of your skills and experience to someone else. You have helped them to grow in their job and when the time is right for your promotion, you can say that there is someone capable of taking your place. Thus both you and your subordinate will benefit from the training you give.

The failure to relax and be sociable in the office

'She's quite a performer and great at her job, but she never smiles.' Do you really want that said of you? Reaping the rewards of business can be particularly tough for women and it's all too easy to get locked into working so hard at your career that you sacrifice other aspects of yourself. If the mirror on your wall says that you're the most serious of them all, then try to relax, even if it's just a little. An occasional smile won't crack the glass and, if nothing else, it'll make your working life more enjoyable. Also, have you ever noticed how much time senior managers spend talking to colleagues, subordinates and business contacts? Statistics indicate that some managers spend as much as two-thirds of their work hours in this activity. How else can they find out how things are going in their departments? Social skills become increasingly important the higher up you move.

Joyce, for instance, owns a printing company and is in frequent contact with clients to review their orders and reservice their supplies. Her business is successful and her service is excellent. However, no one ever feels relaxed in her presence because she maintains such a stiff distant manner in all her business meetings. This makes the atmosphere very uncomfortable and the average buyer wants to finish the meeting with Joyce and get out of there in a hurry.

Joyce is a good businesswoman, and her failure to relax hasn't lost her any customers yet. But it might in the future and meanwhile she isn't enjoying her work contacts as much as she might.

Here are some tell-tale indicators of awkward behaviour which tend to put a damper on office socialization. If you recognize any of these traits in yourself, do make an effort to get rid of them.

Negative body language
Be aware of any mannerisms you may have, particularly those that suggest you are feeling fed up or impatient, either with an individual or the drift of a meeting. For instance, try to avoid nail biting, smoking or fiddling noisily or sighing or 'tsking' under your breath. Don't rustle papers or stand up ostentatiously when meetings look as if they're going to be a waste of time. When you do feel it's essential to express your dissatisfaction, do so in a simple, straightforward way without any of these accompanying gestures, otherwise your colleagues and superiors may think you don't like them, or the company, or even that you're unhappy with your job. For obvious reasons this is a dangerous impression to create.

If you know that it's difficult for you to regain your composure once you have been put out by something someone has said or done, take five deep, slow breaths. This isn't a joke. It gives you a chance to recover your cool and think of what you are going to say so that it doesn't come out sounding emotional or angry. Aim to create a pleasant humorous and accommodating persona without being flabby or weak. Remember your body language often creates more effect than the words coming out of your mouth.

Becoming inaccessible or isolated

As women move into managerial positions, they sometimes feel that there is no more time for chit-chat. To some extent they may be reacting to the fact that women who are too casual in their behaviour at work are likely to be accused of being gossipy and, therefore, not serious about their jobs. However, the reverse also holds some stiff penalties.

Becoming inaccessible in the social context of the workplace is to be cut off from the grapevine. So spend a bit of time around the cafeteria, reception area and cloakroom. These are the places where people congregate and often let slip useful snippets of information. It's a way, for instance, of finding out whether your decisions are having any impact; are you getting positive feedback about them from fellow workers?

If you're having a working lunch you don't have to launch straight into the business – it makes you seem dauntingly serious. Give yourself and everyone else time to relax and talk informally; listening to people telling you about their hobbies and way of life can be very revealing about their personalities.

Cultivating good relationships in your working life will make your job more fun and more interesting; it also oils the wheels of advancement. If the choice lies between two people with similar qualifications and roughly equal experience but one has a charming, outgoing personality, whereas the other seems rather aloof and taciturn, the odds are that the more sociable character will get the job.

Consolidating your personal support system

In chapter 3 we mentioned briefly how important it is to assess your domestic arrangements and prepare yourself to make better provisions against the time when you are offered an exciting new job or promotion. It's very important to be well organized on the home front because you won't be able to do your job properly if you are constantly worrying about what's going on at home. This sounds so obvious it shouldn't need telling, but it's surprising how many women try to get by somehow on somewhat *ad hoc* arrangements and then suffer agonies of guilt, especially when things go wrong.

Balancing all aspects of your life is essential to personal fulfilment. A leading business school impresses on all its students the importance of recognizing and harmonizing these three priorities equally: your work, your self and your family and friends.

Unfortunately, state provision for working mothers is still very minimal in Britain, especially when we compare what is on offer with some of our European neighbours. Here, it's left to women to make their own arrangements, and largely pay for them, since we have few State (or workplace) crèches and nursery schools.

If you are married and have a family you may decide that more help is essential. An *au pair* arrangement may have worked perfectly adequately while the children were small and you were taking a career break, but someone more professional and committed is needed if you intend to return to a full-time career. The trained nanny, whether she comes to your home on a daily basis or lives in, is expensive but probably worth every penny for the peace of mind she will give you. Another cheaper possibility, at least while your children are very small, is to put them in the care of a registered child-minder (see Further Reading for some helpful books on making childcare arrangements).

To decide what kind of personal support system you need, your best bet is to sit down, by yourself, and make a full and realistic review of your commitments and capabilities both at home and at work. Then discuss your needs with your husband.

A well-organized personal support system for women with children should include at its most basic:

1. Sufficient back-up care for children after school. And don't forget the school holidays!

2. Arrangements for someone to take care of a child should illness strike.

3. Ditto, for your out-of-town trips.

4. A discussion – preferably in advance – with your boss regarding situations that might require you to leave the office early or arrive late.

5. A reliable on-going arrangement for help with work you

can't always do yourself; for example, cleaning, cooking or other housekeeping duties.

There are many ways to build a good support system. It is to be hoped that your partner shares the domestic work with you, but if not, or if neither of you has much time, then you may have to hire professional help for some household duties. Don't, for heaven's sake, feel guilty about it, and don't let anyone else try to make you feel bad either. Stay-at-home friends can sometimes try to suggest that a mother's duty is to be a mother twenty-four hours a day. That's probably how you feel too, but it doesn't mean you have to be there, physically, all the time.

If you've got a mother or mother-in-law living nearby who is active and doesn't mind being called upon, then be grateful for your good fortune. Another possibility is share and share-about with a friend who has children of the same age.

Your family and its happiness are sure to be the most important concerns in your life, so it's hardly sensible to spend a lot of your time at work worrying about not being able to keep up with the routine work required to keep any family going. As with your job, you must learn to delegate tasks in order to make the best use of the time you spend with your family.

Success and the single woman

It's just as important for the woman on her own to develop a strong personal support system. She needs to have a few close friends outside her work environment, some interests that are completely unrelated to work, and the sure knowledge that if some accident or disaster were to befall her, she would know who to call on for help.

Start by establishing a solid home base, a place to call your own. It's obviously wise to get into the property market as soon as you can because this is a way of building up capital, helped by the tax relief you get on your mortgage. Avoid getting so caught up by your work that you never have time to go to a film, or a theatre, or entertain a few people at home.

You may prefer not to have a live-in companion or lover but this doesn't stop you from forming close personal relationships with men and women. Your friends will see you through the bad times as well as the good, especially if you are prepared to do the same for them. It's very comforting to know that someone who cares about you is there to water your plants, feed your pet, take care of any possible emergencies while you're away, or just be ready to listen when you need to talk. Friends can also help to counteract any unhealthy tendency to workaholism, if that's something to which you're prone.

On a practical level all women, single or married, should make a point of learning about credit, insurance and pension schemes, investment and how to secure personal loans. A good relationship with your bank is an invaluable asset, so get on good terms with your bank manager. And if you suspect you're never going to hit it off with him, or her, then find another. In the long run it will be less of a hassle to change your bank than to deal with an unsympathetic manager.

A good support system for the single woman includes:

1. A stable, permanent home base;
2. Developing strong personal relationships;
3. Acquiring some financial know-how and consolidating it by being on good terms with your bank manager.

Politics, communication, quality, visibility and timing

We've talked in this chapter about some of the self-inflicted problems women sometimes bring upon themselves. Let's examine how they tie in with the factors that affect advancement.

The failure to relax and be sociable in the office relates most to politics. If you become driven to set over-high standards, for yourself as much as for others, you risk upsetting the balance of the job in hand by being preoccupied with sheer efficiency to such an extent that you distort the true nature of the task and ignore the needs of the people involved in doing it with you.

Socializing from time to time takes the pressure off and is an effective way of gaining political perspective on office work and relationships. It improves communication all round, giving you a chance to indicate informally some of your wants and needs as well as hearing those of others. It shows that you are interested in other people and enjoy their company. It also pays politically to fit into the pace and style of the organization in which you work, rather than attempting to change everything overnight. So, take time to cement good relationships with your fellow workers and bring a relaxed and sociable persona to your daily work.

Good communication is also vital to successful delegation. It gives you a chance to show your respect for other people and your appreciation of their endeavours. Always give them as much positive feedback as possible.

Quality matters too when you are delegating work. A subordinate may not do as quick or thorough a job at a routine task as you would but the delegation itself may enable you to devote more time and care to another significant project. An over-attention to routine details may prevent you from seeing the larger picture – an important part of any manager's work.

Visibility is always enhanced by a relaxed and confident social manner. The more people you know and take the time to talk and listen to, the higher your profile will be. And if the time you spend with them is pleasant as well as productive, the more positive that profile will be.

Timing will determine when you delegate, when you don't: a subordinate who is working on one difficult new project shouldn't be saddled with another. Similarly, a colleague rushing to meet a deadline may not want to have a casual sociable conversation just at that moment. Exercise your judgement and your tact in such situations.

Before filling out the worksheet that concludes this chapter, take a look at the 'Report Card on Women's Progress in Business'. This is what Ruth calls her tongue-in-cheek view of women's general strengths and weaknesses in the workplace, but try grading your own personal performance against these criteria.

REPORT CARD ON WOMEN'S PROGRESS IN BUSINESS

Learning all skills related to job description	Excellent
Ability to interact with boss and be a team player	Satisfactory
Motivation to acquire new management skills for advancement	Excellent
Ability to groom a successor	Fail
Ability to use opportunities to delegate	Fail
Ability to integrate social qualities with task management	Needs improvement
Ability to select activities in the community and in the organization that enhance visibility	Satisfactory
Ability to play office politics and gain access to informal information systems	Needs improvement
Ability to socialize and be at ease with clients, colleagues and suppliers	Needs improvement

Delegation

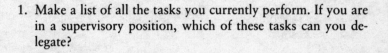

1. Make a list of all the tasks you currently perform. If you are in a supervisory position, which of these tasks can you delegate?

2. Take one task and break it down into its components.

    1.
    2.
    3.
    4.
    5.

3. Is there someone working for you who has the experience and skill to perform this task?

4. If not, is there someone who appears to want more responsibility, who has suggested a different way of carrying out the task or who could benefit from the experience of performing the task?

5. Based on your answers to questions 3 and 4, select a person to whom you want to delegate the task.

6. Set a date to commence training this person, as well as dates for completing training in each component of the task as listed in question 2. Thus:

Starting date:

Completion date for Component 1:

Component 2:

Component 3:

Component 4:

Component 5:

Grooming a successor

1. List the basic tasks that are essential to anyone in your position.

2. Using the same criteria as those in questions 3 and 4 in the preceding questions on delegation, select a person to groom as your successor.

3. Calculate the time you will need on a weekly basis to train this person in the basic tasks.

4. As with delegation, set starting and completion dates for each stage in the training.

Sources of support

1. In attempting to integrate your work, personal and family life, take a look at the following people in your life and determine how they can be helpful to you and how often.

	Partner	Parents/ Family	Children	Boss/ Colleagues	Friends
	Tasks	Tasks	Tasks	Tasks	Tasks
Daily					
Weekly					
Occasional					
Specific					
Never					

2. If you don't have enough help, can you hire someone for specific tasks, e.g. babysitters, housekeepers, etc?

3. Can you trade responsibilities with neighbours and friends?

4. Have you checked neighbourbood cooperatives or support groups to find out what services are available to you?

5. Keep a complete list handy of your personal support system, both at home and at the office. The list should include the names, addresses and business and home telephone numbers of:
   1. Your partner
   2. Close friend or neighbour
   3. Your parents
   4. Your children's school(s)
   5. Doctor
   6. Lawyer
   7. Accountant
   8. Insurance agent
   9. Other (e.g., relatives who can help in a crisis, babysitters, housekeepers, etc.)

Summary

* Take stock of your olds habits, good and bad. Which ones need changing?
* Remember the social side of business
* Look at your work and your staff to determine which tasks you can delegate and to whom
* Work on training a replacement
* Consolidate your personal support system

5

Go!
How to Get There from Here

Two people may have identical jobs within an organization, the same qualifications and responsibilities, similar experience, and both hold a good track record, yet they may advance in entirely different ways. To a casual observer it may look as if one person's advancement over another's is a matter of chance – of being in the right place at the right time. In some cases this is true but there are people who consistently succeed in finding themselves in the right place at the right time *because they have taken specific steps to be there*. What looks like luck is often the result of careful planning. Even women themselves who ascribe their success to luck are surprised when it is pointed out to them that their own natural good instincts for politics, timing and acquiring skills have been crucial in getting them where they are.

In this chapter we will be taking the mystery out of 'being in the right place at the right time'. Women tend to concentrate so hard on job performance that they ignore all the 'incidental' aspects of their work as, for instance, socializing, seeking out a mentor, or discovering what benefits are available to them through their own organizations. To treat these and other activities at work as casual, unimportant factors in advancement is to stack the cards against yourself right from the start. Acquiring skills which may not be directly related to your present job, or learning the art of negotiation, for example, are so important that we are devoting entire chapters to them.

It is quite essential to integrate *all* strategies of your plan for getting to the top. Chapter 3 dealt mainly with performing well in your present position; chapter 4 with recognizing some of the most common pitfalls in the paths of working women; this chapter will focus on the steps you can take to prepare yourself for advancement.

Indicating your interest in advancement and your willingness to be mobile

In chapter 3 we mentioned the importance of letting your boss know that you want to advance. That alone, however, is not enough: you must show it in your actions as well as in words. Sometimes these actions involve politics and too many women tend to regard 'politicking' as indulging in something rather disreputable, or, at the very least, as an unproductive waste of time.

Kate, for instance, is an ambitious university professor with an interest in research and an impressive history of published work. She knows that research and writing are essential credits for a professional in today's highly competitive academic job market, and yet her reluctance to participate in politics gives her fellow professors and the head of her department the impression that she is not interested in getting ahead.

Kate's problem is that she loathes the politically charged departmental meetings in which professors are assigned new graduate students working on research. These students can be a tremendous help to a researcher, carrying out studies and compiling data. And yet Kate is so quiet at the meetings that she often gets only one graduate student, while others less involved in research get three or four.

The immediate result of this is that Kate has less help with her work. She is therefore less productive than she could be and has less time for her family. Quite as serious, she gives her colleagues and superiors the impression that she is content to work away at her research without the help or stimulation of enthusiastic students. The completely unintentional message of her behaviour in departmental meetings is a lack of excitement about her work – and about her own advancement.

Even if you don't like the idea of 'wasting time' at extra

meetings, or helping out with someone else's work, or letting people know how excited you are about a particular project, doing so is as clear a way of telling people you want to advance as actually saying the words – and sometimes it is even more effective.

One issue that may arise in your career is the possibility of a promotion involving a move. Are you willing to relocate in order to move up? If so, make it clear to the people who will be making the decision.

Committing yourself to learning and practising interpersonal skills

While the word 'politics' tends to have a negative connotation, one of its components is totally positive and underlies all the strategies for advancement suggested in this book: good interpersonal skills. People gain tremendous credibility by expressing themselves clearly, concisely and with consistency. Once you reach a high level of responsibility it's particularly important for you to realize that your own achievements depend on the efforts of others. If you are failing to communicate well with your staff or not inspiring them to carry through your plans, then you are the one who is ultimately going to suffer.

Interdependence between colleagues, and between managers and subordinates, is an inescapable reality of organizational life. Consequently, as we showed in chapter 3, the drive towards learning how to be a team player has never been so strong, or so necessary. Essentially, good team playing involves interacting well with the other members of the team; in short, having well-developed interpersonal skills. If you lack these skills, your team performance will be crippled and if you fail to understand the human dynamics of certain team situations, the costs could be high.

Consider, for instance, that as a matter of course you can expect to encounter differences of opinion among members of your team. Do you have the skills to deal with them? Depending upon how you handle these conflicts, they can either hinder your progress through the organization or add momentum to your achievement. Because women have been conditioned to fear conflict, they have a tendency to back off from confrontation and become constant, behind-the-scenes complainers instead. But complaining on a regular basis is not productive: it wastes time, it's negative and disagreeable to hear and, even though it may be justified, people begin to perceive the moaner as a nuisance. There's a very important lesson here: people who complain in organizations may be listened to, but they don't get promoted. A positive approach to problems, whether they be practical or interpersonal, always produces better results.

If you can learn to handle conflict positively, the effects on your career can be almost miraculous. Take the story of Gloria, an efficient office manager in a large firm of chartered surveyors. There are several partners and every time Gloria needs to make a major purchase of office equipment they must all be consulted. The problem for Gloria is that they are a busy team and she finds it hard to pin them down to a decision.

Her initial strategy was to approach each boss separately with her request for approval. Inevitably the decision would be postponed because the group couldn't agree among itself and Gloria would grumble, to her bosses and her subordinates, about not being able to get on with her job. Finally, she decided to take the bull by the horns, so to speak.

Gloria took the first steps in initiating the purchasing by soliciting bids from a number of companies on the various equipment options. Then she wrote a summary of these bids with her preferences and requested a meeting of the complete management team to discuss her proposal. This proved successful in more ways than one. It promoted her not only as an initiator but also as someone who was capable of dealing with potential conflict and increased responsibility. She is now included more often in management decision-making.

We shall be saying more about conflict in chapter 9, but here, to be getting on with, are a few tips on how to deal with it:

1. In office disagreements, learn to listen before you act. Many times in situations of conflict, we don't allow the other party to explain their position. Learning to listen forces you to appreciate fully the facts as they appear to your 'opponents'. Moreover, just

showing that you are willing to listen is often enough to heal the wounds – real or imaginary – they feel they have suffered.

2. As a gesture of respect, arrange to meet adversaries alone before airing your differences publicly. If you handle conflict privately it has a much greater chance of being contained before it turns into a major breach.

3. Remember that conflict does not always have to produce a winner. Indeed, it is best resolved when both sides win. This is possible when some interests of both parties can be accommodated. If the scale is too heavily weighted in favour of a 'victor', feelings of resentment tend to linger in the air and these can surface later over other issues. Nowhere is this more true than in negotiation, where both sides must generally give and take. We will be dealing with this particularly crucial problem in chapter 8.

There's another element in team playing that can be downright dangerous, so if you find yourself in these deep waters, advance warily. Sometimes team projects require 'underground' activities – a polite way of saying that you may be expected to doctor the facts. If you find yourself in this situation you have only two choices: go along with it or protest.

Women have had less experience of management than men and they may not like some of the rules men have made, nor some of the 'dirty tricks' they play. When you suspect that a certain situation is rather dubious – for example, making the company's profit position look a little rosier than it really is – ask yourself whether you are being commercially naive, over-scrupulous or whether indeed you have good reason to be worried about the ethics of such behaviour.

Whatever your feelings, *don't* communicate them to the team until you have discussed your point of view with an outsider, say a close friend whose opinion you trust, or a respected mentor. You may be advised that it makes sense to toe the team line rather than to make a big deal out of a small – and common – business practice. However, if the situation really is serious and you feel that your personal morality and integrity are being compromised, you should request an open review of the situation and take the risk that you will end up either alienated from the team or thrown off it. There is, of course, the other more constructive possibility: that your courage in confronting the issue will help others, who are similarly concerned but are too timid to express their doubts, to come forward and give you their support.

Cultivating a mentor

The dictionary defines a mentor as an 'experienced trusted adviser'. In a business situation a mentor is someone who has already been where you want to go and who is willing to take you under their wing. Their previously successful negotiation of the territory should ensure that their guidance will be reliable and that they can provide you with accurate interpretations of potentially tricky situations.

A mentor is one of the best insurance policies a successful career person can have. His or her contribution to the professional advancement of more junior men and women has been well documented. As Daniel Levinson writes in his book *The Seasons of a Man's Life*: 'A mentor can act as a teacher to enhance skills and intellectual development, as a sponsor to facilitate entry and advancement, as a host and guide, welcoming the initiate into a new occupational and social world, acquainting him or her with its values and customs. A mentor is also an exemplar the protégé can admire and emulate, and someone who provides moral support in time of stress.'

A mentor can be enormously beneficial to a woman on her way up. He or she can give her a good understanding of the texture of the organization in which she works, its culture and history, as well as a sense of what events have been – or are – significant in its growth. Perhaps more importantly, a mentor can make her aware of which people in the organization will play a significant role in her advancement, and act as a link with them.

Consider, for instance, the story of Louise, who began her career at twenty-two as an assistant sales person in a book publishing firm. She had been hired directly by the chairman, an older man whom she liked enormously and who would be retiring in five years' time. He created a job for her because he was impressed by her energy and intelligence and he was looking for new blood to inject into his flagging company. She had only been in this position for six months when the position of promotion manager became vacant. Louise suggested to the chairman that he allow her to have a crack at it. Although she had few managerial skills and no direct experience, he put her into the position on a trial basis for three months.

During that time he taught her about the business, guided her through the bad and difficult times and helped her understand the dynamics of company politics. Because she respected his experience and wisdom, she flourished. She was also careful not to excite the jealousy of her colleagues by being too obviously in his pocket. Over the next five years she turned her department into one of the most successful of its kind in the country, and the company's sales increased accordingly. Her relationship with the chairman blossomed and he became proud of her in a fatherly way. During this period he also confided a number of his business problems to her, and she tried to help him overcome them.

They both benefited from this mutual support. Louise advanced into a business of her own, knowing that she would never have been able to take this step so soon and so confidently without a mentor of her boss's capacity. He retired with the satisfaction of having turned his company around.

As you have seen from Louise's case, the advantages which come from choosing your mentor wisely can be enormous. There are, however, some potential pitfalls to beware of. For one thing, it's dangerous to become totally dependent on a single relationship. What happens if you have a falling out with your mentor, or he or she falls from grace within the organization or leaves the company? You mustn't put yourself into a position where you are forced to deny your mentor because that will make you look very disloyal – not an attractive thing to be – so you must learn to tread a fine line between regard for your mentor's position and looking after your own tail. This self-interest means that you must constantly reassess whether your mentor's power base is broad enough to support the kind of advancement you have in mind for yourself; you must also be sure that you are not blocking other opportunities for yourself by relying so exclusively on one person for advice and guidance.

Tracey, for example, found that by putting all her eggs in one basket she ended up with none. Her boss had nurtured her through her training as an accountant and seen that she was regularly promoted. However, after eight years he sidestepped in the company to an area she had no wish to enter. She found herself with little work – his clients had been distributed among the other partners – and in the vulnerable position of being a pseudo 'new girl' who had to establish relations with these partners.

If your mentor is a male, be careful about letting your relationship become a sexual one, however tempting it may be. The business and bed mix, whether with a mentor or a colleague, is risky at best, disastrous at worst. It can wreak havoc with your working relationship, cause problems and gossip in the office, and could ultimately have a calamitous effect on your career. The corridors of power are littered with the remains of women who allowed their emotions to get the best of them and broke this cardinal rule. The fact that the same does not apply to men just means, as women know only too well, that life isn't fair. We haven't yet been able to abolish this double standard, and won't until there are many more women in senior positions. While it exists, don't risk your future flouting it: the game is not worth the candle if you are serious about geting to the top.

Patricia, for instance, worked as a consultant in a large management consulting firm. One of her colleagues was a man in a senior position whom she liked very much and found interesting to talk to. They began to spend lunch hours together in the company gym. Fairly soon, Patricia felt herself feeling sexually attracted to this man and knew that he felt the same towards her. She made certain that her lunch hour coincided with his, and whenever possible she also ran into him on her way home so that they could have a drink and talk about their business day. The encounters soon led to bed.

However, after two weeks of intense love-making her lover

began to withdraw. He no longer came to the gym and working with him became strained and awkward. They couldn't get back to the original colleague basis and Patricia felt uncomfortable talking to him about anything because she sensed that he was rejecting her sexually. She, meanwhile, had not resolved her own feelings for him. After a month of this turmoil she could bear it no longer. She left her excellent position in her company because the emotional trauma was seriously affecting her work.

Look before you leap. A good relationship with a mentor on a business or social level can be tremendously satisfying and rewarding for both sides, as it was in Louise's case. Anything else is a great risk, not only to your career but to your emotional stability and well-being.

There is another less obvious way in which a relationship with a mentor can be detrimental. As writer Henry Weil recently pointed out in the American magazine, *Savvy*: 'If the mentor tried to cover up a subordinate's flaws, sooner or later his shortcomings surfaced anyway. Conversely, even when one subordinate was truly talented, he was often perceived as overly dependent on his mentor, and denied promotion as a result.'

This reinforces our earlier point that it is very important to choose your mentor wisely and keep a balanced view about his or her place in your life. Mentors should be viewed objectively as resources in a specific space and time. They may well outlive their usefulness in the business environment which does not mean that you can't continue to have a good relationship with them in your personal or social life.

Participating in voluntary activities and social events

Communicating your desire to move onward and upward can be achieved not only through professional commitments but also through voluntary work. Participating in social events, charities, community committee work, competitions and other activities shared by people in the upper echelons of your organization will heighten your visibility and identify you as a person with similar interests; you will be rated as an agreeable member of the company team.

The informal relationships that often result from this participation can reap specific professional rewards, such as new contacts and access to information about future openings or new developments in the organization. We British who tend to be a bit shy about offering ourselves in this kind of capacity should take a leaf out of our transatlantic cousins' book. Generally speaking, they have far fewer inhibitions about being thought 'pushy' or self-seeking; if they see an advantage, they go for it, arguing rightly that if you don't, others will.

Michelle, for instance, is a twenty-six-year-old junior lawyer working in an international legal firm. Due to the company's size, she has little contact with any of the senior partners. Recently, however, a senior partner became chairman of the area health authority. Michelle volunteered as a legal consultant to one of the district hospital committees and quickly earned a good reputation as a leader and spokeswoman on medico-legal issues. Later in the year a key assignment came up in the firm and the senior partner who had seen Michelle in action at the hospital requested her participation.

Every little bit helps!

Socializing with clients, colleagues and suppliers

If you can learn to do this easily and with pleasure you will find that it is a wonderful way of keeping your fingers on the pulse of the industry in which you work. And should the time come when you want to leave your present job, you can put the word around discreetly so that these acquaintances can tip you off when someone leaves a company or they hear of a new job opening up which sounds right for you. Quite often it happens that someone's talent is more quickly recognized outside the organization in which they work, so they may be head-hunted into another job, or enjoy an experience rather like Charlotte's.

Charlotte used to work as director of personnel in a large chain of gift and stationery stores. She had a very high profile within the national retailers' association and various personnel associations. Interestingly, the people in her own company regarded her as competent but viewed her external commitments (which she made sure didn't eat into her working time) as being those of someone who just wanted to be in the limelight. During a recent merger of her organization with a similar business, however, Charlotte was the only member of the old management team to be invited to be part of the new leadership of the company: she was the only one known outside the company.

Remember what we said in chapter 3 about the importance of getting connected and networking. As long as your involvement is not so time-consuming that it affects your performance at work, such an organization can be a marvellous source of support, friendship and information. If you haven't already joined an association or group which has some relevance to your work, think again and consult our Resource List on pages 219–226.

Becoming aware of the new technology

Each industry has its own changing technology. In most businesses today that technology involves tools such as word processors, computers (both small and massive) and related software.

Many women who have technical backgrounds have fallen into the trap of assuming that their mastery of the new microtechnology will in itself be enough to guarantee success in the workplace. This is a mistake: these women still have to develop the social and practical skills necessary for advancement, otherwise they will be left behind operating the hard- and software but not actually getting involved in the policy-making of the company. They should also be using those skills to ease others' potential discomfort with the new technology.

A second group consists of those who think they can get away with saying that the new technology is too specialized and complex, or that it is irrelevant to their specific jobs. Others, even more self-defeatingly, claim that they are too old to acquire new technological skills. This myth can no longer be upheld. We have all got to develop more positive attitudes – and the skills themselves – when we consider how rapidly and pervasively the new technology is spreading throughout corporations, government and businesses of all sizes.

Rita thought this way until the day her company, a paper products manufacturer, informed Rita and her fellow purchasing agents that it had decided that they would be more efficient if they installed microcomputers. Rita, who is in her fifties and considered she had managed perfectly well without them for the last thirty years, was at first terrified that she would never be able to master the new technology. It's true that by comparison with people twenty years younger than herself she did take a bit longer to get the hang of it, but once she had, she became fascinated by what it could do for her and now she can't understand how she ever managed without her computer. All Rita did to achieve this skill was to attend the courses arranged for her by the company, but she brought to them an unshakeable determination that 'no one is going to say I'm too old to learn. . . '.

An eager, hands-on attitude to the new technology will put you in a more favourable position when promotions are granted or at points of hiring in new companies. If you want to be on the fast track, this is one of the basic areas for training. Start by finding out what's on offer inside your company. If there's little or nothing available, make enquiries at your local polytechnic or college of further education, and if you do find a good basic course, ask your company to sponsor you on it, or pay for it yourself if you can't honestly claim that it's relevant to your present job. In chapter 7 we will be dealing in more depth with the kind of skills you should be acquiring and how to select courses.

Learning about benefit plans associated with different management levels

You should be asking questions that relate to company benefits long before your next promotion is due. Most people visit the personnel departments of their organizations their first day on the job, when they fill out various application forms, for a pension and so on, and then never go back. This is bad practice, as there are times when, say, your salary may be commensurate with the job but you are missing out on perks which other employees in your grade have managed to secure for themselves.

Fiona is a credit supervisor in a department store where she has been working for ten years since she left school. She is well regarded by her colleagues and the clients with whom she deals; indeed, her boss thinks she is the most expert, reliable and capable member of his team. But Fiona is the only one who hasn't got a company car.

She has never asked for one because she hates talking about money and what she calls 'playing at office politics'. In this case it would mean pointing out that her three male colleagues who do have cars have received preferential treatment and she doesn't want to make anyone feel uncomfortable. Needless to say, this shrinking-violet attitude is just fine with management. Even when she had an opportunity to redress the situation and re-negotiate the terms of her employment following a company merger, Fiona couldn't bring herself to ask for what was her due, and this despite her new boss pointing out the inequity of the situation. Since she didn't act on his prompting, he assumed, after waiting six months, that she didn't want to improve her benefit package, and let the whole matter lapse.

Fiona's mistake is to call this kind of negotiation 'politics' instead of seeing it for what it is – namely, looking after her own interests. If she continues to be so delicate about negotiating her compensation packages, she is soon going to be way behind her colleagues which won't do her any good in the long run, quite apart from undermining her sense of self-esteem. Like a lot of women, she will continue to work hard and expect the company to take care of her. The sooner she realizes that there is no company knight in shining armour to protect and reward her, the better off she will be.

The moral to draw from this sad story is that if you want more, and it is realistic to expect it, then *ask* for it, even if, unlike Fiona, you're not always entirely sure that you are worth it. The world is a tough place and you have to fight for what you want. You will need different benefits at different stages in your life, and you should know ahead of time how these are distributed in your company. Many employees have standard packages as well as individual options. It is important for you to learn how to coordinate your benefits with your own personal needs, or, if you are married, with your husband's benefits. Also, don't forget to review and update your policies at least once a year and always on the occasion of a promotion. If renegotiation is possible, you should make every effort to improve your package. Corporate negotiation is the same kind of activity on a grander scale, and we will be dealing with its complexities in chapter 8.

Politics, communication, quality, visibility and timing

There *are* rare occasions when quality alone is rewarded, but most of the time it goes hand in hand with using a bit of political nous. Emma's story is a good example of the way these qualities can be combined to excellent effect.

For several years she has been the personnel manager of a large retail company which has four hundred outlets throughout the country. At one point, she was unable to fill the position of manager for one of the smaller showpiece shops which happened to be near the head office, so she took on the responsibility for it herself. Emma did this for eight months, and, because she was so efficient about absorbing it into her other activities, the company began to assume that she would continue to do it without compensation. This she was not prepared to do. She requested a change in her job description and title and put a time limit on her performing the two functions. She also negotiated extra money and continued as before for another three months, by which time she had trained up a suitable replacement.

Emma was well liked in her company and there was no doubt that she was a competent manager. In addition, her visibility and political skills were exceptional so when the job of personnel director, a senior management position, fell vacant through retirement, the chairman and board of directors had no hesitation in offering her the post, even though she was still relatively young.

Certainly Emma was fortunate that her management believe in recognizing and rewarding quality, irrespective of whether it comes from men or women. It still happens that women have to perform twice as well and work twice as hard to get the recognition they deserve. One way of overcoming this problem is never to let slip an opportunity for renegotiation. Emma's handling of her situation shows how necessary it is to know what compensation packages are available to you, but information on its own is not enough; acting on it at the right moment (timing) is critical. And negotiation, what Fiona dismissed as 'playing at politics', will probably also be necessary to achieve success.

Communication goes hand in hand with visibility as part of the strategy for progress. For instance, it's crucial to keep your accomplishments and those of your subordinates in the front line. If, from time to time, you generously share that front line with your boss and your peers, then they will usually do the same for you. Conversely, if you never acknowledge the contributions of others they will develop an underlying distrust of you.

Taking credit for your accomplishments is essential. Women tend to be shy of asserting their ownership of ideas or projects, with the result that they often end up losing control over what has been initiated by them. All reports and documents that you initiate should carry your name and the date, as well as the name of the person to whom they are being presented. This doesn't guarantee that you will be the ultimate spokesperson or supervisor for the issue, but it does record the fact that the initiative was yours.

Sheila, for instance, was an experienced social worker, newly appointed to the cerebral palsy unit of a large district hospital. Her case load included working with the families of children who had this disability. Sheila was a firm believer in the value of group counselling, a technique for which she had had lengthy training, and she wanted to organize such a group with these families. She eagerly informed the consultant paediatrician of her view and he, liking the idea, subsequently brought it up at a medical meeting to which Sheila had not been invited. A registrar offered to run the group and without further ado the consultant gave him the responsibility. Sheila was furious, but the experience taught her an important lesson:

always document your ideas and make crystal clear what part you wish to play in their implementation.

Sheila should have written a proposal to the doctor, along the following lines:

1. A description of what the programme involved and a complete list of the clients from her current case load who could benefit from it.

2. A full description of her own professional training and experience in the field.

3. A list of services she would need from other hospital departments, as well as suggestions for handling the coordination.

4. A statement of how she saw her responsibility for recording the development of this service and making recommendations for its future growth.

Communication sometimes does involve blowing your own trumpet. You may find the notion distasteful, but unless you discard false modesty and present yourself and your accomplishments in a straightforward manner to those who are in a position to make use of them, you aren't going to get ahead as far as you would wish.

Quality in the workplace relates basically to meeting accepted company standards about various aspects of work: for example, it could be a matter of presentation to a client; the depth of background research put into evaluating a new project; or the careful follow-up of a marketing exercise. Quality is based on a subjective assessment; what you, your boss or your company rates as high quality may be three quite different standards.

If it matters a lot to you to be a perfectionist then don't work for a business which makes its money by turning over large quantities of cheap goods. If, on the other hand, you subscribe to the view that 'if a thing is worth doing, it's worth doing badly' you will be happier working for an organization which is more concerned with results than how you get them.

When trying to do your own personal quality control exercise the relevant questions to ask yourself are, 'What is enough from me to make a useful contribution?' or, 'Am I putting myself dangerously into overdrive?' The desire to over-achieve and turn in a perfect performance every time is something that many women find hard to moderate, but it is essential if you are going to avoid suffering from burn-out. Remember what we have said in earlier chapters: there is no virtue in being a workaholic and it does make you a bit of a bore.

The importance of visibility in moving up is exemplified by the story of Veena, who started out as a secretary seventeen years ago and is now head of accounting in her company. Finding that figures interested her, she asked to be moved to the accounts department where for some time she did all the routine jobs, but as soon as she had become proficient in one area she asked to be transferred to another. Meanwhile she decided to study at night school for the exams of the Association of Certified Accountants. As soon as she felt sufficiently knowledgeable she volunteered to sit on the audit committee of her company. Her humble duty of taking the minutes nonetheless gave her an opportunity to get to know the treasurer and the chairman who were both senior managers in the organization.

Veena also volunteered to write up the account reports and budgets for other departments. As a result she became visible to the entire organization as someone who was keenly interested in her work and professional in the way she set about it. When the position of head of accounting became vacant Veena was the obvious nominee, so she was offered the job even though she had not quite completed her professional exams.

In her case, visibility had played a crucial part in securing her advancement, as did her sound sense of timing. She didn't volunteer for the audit committee until she knew she could handle it. Careful timing will control your natural enthusiasm and enhance your judgement, so make sure you understand the time framework in which new assignments, positions and pro-motions are distributed.

In many organizations there are formal periods when planning and budgetary preparation occur. Sally worked in a public library in which the establishment of a children's section was announced during a planning meeting. She acted immediately, telling the chief librarian that she would like to head up this section. She was successful in her application and was, therefore, involved in the planning of the new division because her timing had been spot on.

When you start looking ahead to where you want to be, you are entering new vistas of hope, ideas, guts and risks. This positive orientation towards moving up offers as much prospect for success as do experience and lengthy service. By demonstrating this active commitment in all the ways we have suggested in this chapter – learning the new technology, understanding the art of self-promotion, measuring the quality and quantity of your performance, to name a few – you are making yourself an attractive investment. Those with the power to promote you will feel encouraged by your energy and initiative and be convinced that you are a good risk to back.

WORKSHEET 5

Cultivating a Mentor

1. Which people in your organization have key information about specific tasks you want to learn, new jobs, reorganization, corporate changes in direction or political developments?

2. Do you work directly with any of these people, or happen to get along with them?

3. If so, do you work on developing your relationship with any of them by asking questions, being visible, taking initiatives or showing interest in specific aspects of their work?

4. If not, what aspects of your job might naturally lead you to make contact with them and start developing a relationship?

5. Having chosen a mentor, define what you have to offer them and what you want to learn from them.

6. Have you made sure that you aren't isolating yourself from other colleagues by building an exclusive relationship with one mentor?

Summary

* Work on your interpersonal skills
* Cultivate business contacts and mentors
* Keep abreast of the new technology
* Create opportunities for visibility

6

Playing the Game

No matter how rewarding your work is, no matter how carefully – and successfully – your career advancement is planned, there will be days when you ask yourself questions like, 'Why am I doing this?' 'Is it all worth it?' or, 'What's in it for me?'

In the last three chapters we have presented a plan for action on several levels. At the core of it, however, is your genuine commitment to a goal. Without that commitment, you are only going through the motions of a successful and rewarding career; unless that is resolved it is bound to lead to conflict and disillusionment in the future.

In outlining our plan for moving up we have concentrated on certain important areas of action, the practical steps to put them into effect and the professional benefits to be gained by them. Now we are going to look at the personal side of work: the rewards that make you feel good and which come from bringing your own vision, skills and potential to your career.

We all have to do a certain amount of work we don't enjoy or find immediately useful. However, if we can maintain a level, objective perspective on these humdrum, day-to-day tasks, we will be able also to see the long-term rewards that come from doing them. Bearing this in mind let's examine some of the crucial issues in career work and analyse what they mean to you.

Politics – the larger picture

'Politics revolts but intrigues me,' said one woman interviewed for this book. 'I don't like office politics, I ignore it,' said a second. A third had a more realistic apporach: 'Politics is a way of life . . . I've learned to use grapevines and contacts in the industry to obtain information.'

'Office politics' is still such a dirty phrase in the minds of many women that they forget some of the most important – and positive – aspects of it. We have talked about its usefulness for gaining information and conducting your own negotiations. Now let's think about it in terms of training your conceptual ability, an invaluable skill for every sphere of life.

The ability to conceptualize means that you are able to extract a general meaning or purpose from what may appear to be trivial and disorganized situations and events. It is an abstract mental ability concerned with conceiving and analysing general ideas and concepts; as such it is quite different from the applied intelligence you use when carrying out specific tasks, or even when acquiring a formal training of some sort. In this particular context we are concerned with conceptual foresight, which is the ability to anticipate needs or consequences in a political setting.

Good conceptual skills are essential to success in an organization. They influence your ability to solve problems and make quicker responses to given situations. From a political point of view, they enable you to stand back and look at your organization objectively. You will be able to judge, for instance, whether your superior is sufficiently powerful to attend the important meetings in which all the key people are involved. You will also get an idea of whether he or she is a reliable support to you in aiding your own advancement. Does your boss, for instance, pass on information to you before it is a *fait accompli* so that you can act in anticipation, or are you usually left in the dark?

Conceptual ability goes hand in hand with the ability to be objective about relationships in the organization, and this, politically speaking, is an invaluable asset because it enables you to identify the power bases in your organization. Who are the traffic cops? Who creates the openings that allow information to flow through the organization, and who tries to block it off? It is also invaluable for helping you to set your own corporate and career goals; and it enables you to understand why it is that you do or do not feel good about your future in the business or company you are working in now.

The following set of questions is designed to help you size up the nature of your organization and your relationship to it. If you have become bogged down in the constant, day-to-day details of your job, you may have been ignoring the more general issues at stake, and these questions should clarify them.

1. Who are the players on the corporate scene?
2. Which issues does the power group rally around?
3. Which company issues are really important to you?
4. Does your company attach the same importance to these issues? If not, can you change things?
5. Do you sympathize with the means and ends of your company?
6. What goals do you wish to achieve within your company?
7. Are they in line with your company's goals?

If your answers to these questions indicate strong conflict between the interests of your company and yourself, then you should be thinking about getting out. Remember, however, that your goals are likely to change over time; they may even have done so quite recently. Also, have you tried to see if the company is receptive to ideas you have for the future – by suggesting strategies and setting dates for specific goals, for example?

If you have been thinking that some of the political strategies we have suggested to you are not really important enough for you to worry about, what about reconsidering them in the context of their larger implications?

Socializing in the office

We have pointed out that mixing with your colleagues informally over lunch or after office hours for a drink is not only one of the pleasures that comes from working in an organization, it's also a good way of ensuring that you're hooked into the office grapevine. However, don't imagine you can absorb information like a piece of blotting paper and not give anything back. You must contribute your share while at the same time keeping a guard on your tongue. During the last war there was a saying:

'Careless talk costs lives'. The same could be said about careers. Use your political nous about what you say to whom and don't confuse chitchat with malicious gossip.

In the larger political context this kind of relaxed social contact enables you to get to know more about the people you work with: their interests, political views, what they do in their private lives. You will begin to understand how they fit into the organization, who the misfits are, and why it is that they don't appear to be right – their fault or the organization's? And how do you yourself slot into the corporate scheme of things? Slowly, that mysterious entity, the company ethos, will begin to make itself apparent to you.

Getting good performance appraisal

The immediate benefits of a good performance appraisal are obvious, which is why we recommend that early on in your plan-making you ask for a copy of the company appraisal form, if there is one, and examine it carefully.

Now take it one step further. If you have an opportunity, take the form to your boss and ask what he or she feels are the most important skills for you to master in your current position. Obviously you will want to focus for the time being on the skills your boss suggests, but think of the other implications of this recommendation. What kinds of skills interest your boss? Are they useful to you, or merely a convenience for the boss? Do they indicate a general direction your boss and company want you to go in? Finally, and most importantly, is it the direction you want for yourself?

Participating in social events and voluntary activities

In chapter 5 we recommend this as a way of gaining useful information both in and outside your company, to enhance your visibility and to build up a network of business contacts. The benefits are equally valuable in the larger context.

First, it should help you to become more comfortable about meeting people generally. Second, the network that grows out of such social activities can be a tremendous source of personal support. You may well develop good, long-lasting friendships in a business network, and that's especially important if you are a busy single career woman living in a large city, possibly far away from your family background.

One general piece of political advice: throughout your career you will meet many different kinds of people. Some will prefer stability, routine and safety in their approach to work. Others will always be generating ideas or stimulating enthusiasm for new projects and ventures. If you are keen on advancement, then seek out the action-oriented people. Their vibrancy will keep you motivated, and when you talk about mobility and moving up, they will back you up. Also, because these are the types who know about taking risks and sometimes failing, they will be supportive to you when you find yourself facing a setback.

As the following story indicates, a good dose of political nous can turn disaster into triumph. Mary was a project manager for a company which, due to a current recession in the industry, had instituted a policy of freezing salaries at their existing levels for a period of two years. Not long after the freeze went into effect, Mary had to hire two new people for her team. Both were less experienced than Mary but the company's hiring policies were more favourable to outsiders than to promoting those within. As a result, these new employees were taken on at salaries that were actually higher than Mary's, even though she was their boss.

Understandably, she was upset and annoyed. She spoke to the regional manager of the company about her predicament, but although he was sympathetic he refused to budge on the company's policy. At first Mary was frustrated and angered by his reaction but, recognizing that the situation was potentially explosive if she didn't handle it properly, she was careful not to show her feelings, nor did she rush into any hasty decisions. Instead, she made the most of her conceptual ability and thought the matter through to come up with an acceptable solution.

She began by requesting two things of her boss: a second meeting with him in two days' time to discuss some alternative proposals, to be followed a week later by a joint meeting with him and her divisional manager. These requests were granted, and in the meantime she consulted some trustworthy colleagues outside her own organization to seek their advice on how to handle the situation. With their help, she devised a sound and simple proposal. She asked that a new title and position be created for her because she was now in charge of a larger staff, and therefore had greater responsibility. This would make her eligible for a salary increase because she would, in effect, be promoted to a new job.

When she formally presented this proposal to her two superiors at the joint meeting she had set up, they were delighted to accede to her request, not least because it was a face-saver for them which had got them out of a tricky situation. They hadn't liked the unfairness of Mary's position; it was not of their making and they certainly didn't want to risk losing her. So, pleasure all round because Mary had got what she wanted for herself, and she collected some credits on the way for her political acumen. We could also call this a fine example of lateral thinking. Incidentally, this is a quality that women are supposed to have in abundance, so use it whenever possible.

On the other hand, a failure to develop a keen political nose can be disastrous. Jane's story illustrates just how badly things can turn out. She was the director of a company division and she was very disturbed by certain changes that were being introduced throughout the company. When head office called a staff development meeting to discuss the changes, Jane, without naming names, made it quite clear that she held her boss at head office responsible for the breakdown in communication between her division and the rest of the company, by having instituted these changes without first consulting her and the other divisional managers. Jane was justified in her complaint but her mistake was to arraign her boss before a hundred members of staff. Everyone felt very uncomfortable because the head office management had been made to look foolish and incompetent.

Jane's ill-considered outburst cost her dear. It had put her into an untenable position because she had lost the confidence of both her own staff and her bosses. Within two months of the incident she had resigned.

The moral of this story is encapsulated by a favourite quotation of Ruth's: 'Among the things we most often open by mistake are our mouths.' Weigh the potential effects of your tongue lashings carefully before you launch into action. In this respect, even the most trivial-seeming political exchange can produce serious long-term problems.

Sex discrimination and sexual harassment

There are some issues that go beyond the internal politics of any organization, and no discussion of working conditions for women could be complete without mentioning sex discrimination and sexual harassment. We all know that both these activities go on inside organizations – indirectly or undercover more often than not – but how to handle the people who practise either is a fairly intractable problem for many women.

Both are illegal and the Equal Opportunities Commission has now taken several employers and individuals to court on behalf of women who have complained that they have been discriminated against in their work or have suffered sexual harassment. Many books have been written about both subjects (see Further Reading) so we don't propose to examine the issues in great detail here.

If, however, you think you have been the victim of any kind of discrimination – indirectly perhaps through not being offered a training course or a promotion to which you consider you are entitled – think hard and carefully before you act. If you belong to a union, consult your branch officer first. Alternatively, write directly to the Equal Opportunities Commission (Overseas House, Quay Street, Manchester M3 3HN) who will consider your case carefully and advise you. If the Commission thinks it merits further investigation, including legal action, it will conduct the case on your behalf.

Sexual harassment is always difficult to handle. You have to distinguish between the teasing or irritating provocation that we all meet and the kind of behaviour that goes beyond the bounds of acceptability. The first can usually be squashed or laughed off, but, with the latter, if you can't put the offender into his place by contempt or ridicule or threatening to report him, consult people whose opinion and advice you value. The last resort is a legal one since, unfortunately, as we have seen from recent sensational news reports, the victim often suffers far more from publicity, humiliation and trauma than the perpetrator.

Enjoyment – the spice of life

No amount of good work, of successful juggling of your personal and professional life, or of swift progress up the career ladder is going to mean anything to you unless you are having some fun along the way.

Are you enjoying yourself? Take the time to consider the following statements:

1. You can loosen up and take a bad day, week, even month in its stride.

2. You feel genuine satisfaction when you perform your work well.

3. You take pride in your reputation as well as in your industry.

4. You give and receive colleague support on new programmes and ventures.

5. You take pleasure in seeing the 'big picture' in your organization as well as the day-to-day events.

6. You are satisfied with the personal support system you have established in order to perform well at your job, whether it's in an organization or running your own business.

If you can answer 'yes' to most of these statements, then you are on the right track. But take a second look at those statements over which you hesitated or had to say an unequivocal 'no'. Do you know why? Is there anything you can do to change things? Is there a thread running through the answers you gave? For instance, you may be having particular trouble in one area, such as your personal support system or your ability to cope with a difficult day.

We all have our own temperaments, tastes and aptitudes. Are yours suited to your work – and vice versa? Sheer enjoyment *is* the spice of life and it's what makes any formula for success work.

Perhaps the best candidate to exemplify the truth of this is the typical entrepreneurial woman. She is likely to be a risk-taker; she is used to promoting herself and she seems able to take the ups and downs of life more easily than some. It may be due to the feeling of freedom that comes from being one's own boss and being able to express one's personality unconstrained by thoughts of conforming to the company image, but certainly many women in this position radiate a sense of enjoyment.

Take Anne, for instance, who is an independent public relations consultant. She thrives on developing her business because her clients, who are in many different fields, enormously widen her own horizons. She has a bubbly charm which serves her well, both with her established clients who always get a lift when they see her and with potential new clients when she is pitching for their account. Her business is small and relatively under-capitalized in relation to some of the giant agencies around, but Anne knows that she always stands a good chance when competing for a new client because of that extra special quality she possesses – a genuinely warm and sympathetic personality.

Anne enjoys being her own boss because it gives her a sense of being in control of her own destiny. Barbara has found a similar degree of enjoyment in creating and developing a new division inside an existing organization. It is a company which manufactures a wide range of health care products. Until Barbara's arrival it had ignored the huge demand for inexpensive physical aids for the elderly. Barbara had just emerged from looking after her elderly mother, who had been severely disabled after a fall. This experience, coupled with Barbara's former training and work as a nurse, enabled her to suggest a comprehensive range of aids which she knew would have a wide market if only they could be manufactured and sold cheaply enough. The chairman, for whom she was then working as a private secretary, was impressed by her proposal and asked her to set up the division. Today, six years later, it is one of the company's most profitable lines.

Barbara loves her work and, like Anne, finds that her energy has been released because of the pleasure she takes in it. She is especially delighted that she could make this successful entry into commerce after twenty years of being a wife and mother. She found that all her well-tried skills of running a large household, making ends meet on a fairly limited housekeeping allowance, and frequently having to mediate between the strong characters gathered under her roof, had taught her a great deal about manageemnt. Picking up the technical know-how when she first started was her main problem, but, like Rita and her computer, she was determined not to be beaten by mere hardware and, very soon, she was perfectly at ease with her subject. Today, she is a leading expert in her field.

These are two success stories. For many women, the struggle to let go and launch themselves into work that they really enjoy is complicated by a number of emotional factors. The conflicts between the demands of the workplace and the home, as well as the excessive guilt which has been programmed into so many women, tend to restrict them from taking the necessary initiatives required to advance. They fear they can't take on any further responsibility at work because it might drain them of the strength they need to cope with their family's demands. They rush off at the end of the day because they haven't arranged the domestic support they need to give them that extra half-hour which they could spend with a colleague to sort out, for example, a problem that has cropped up unexpectedly that day.

This is not to deny that women, particularly those with young families, do have real practical problems to contend with, but if they are serious about getting ahead, they would do well to put a little more thought into ways of easing their burden. Racing around like the White Rabbit, constantly looking at your watch and saying: 'I'm busy, I'm busy,' is actually quite a waste of time. We have talked about the value of social contacts for keeping you informed, but have you also considered that these same contacts can make your life easier, and indeed, save you time?

If, for example, you establish a communication chart on which you identify key contacts in different industries or services and keep this list at your fingertips, you have a whole team of consultants within easy reach when you're confronted with problems and want quick advice. You have to nurture these referral and recommendation sources to keep up the flow of information, so why not do it the nice way by having the odd lunch or after hours drink with them?

Women are not very good at spoiling themselves or at spending time on themselves purely for pleasure. If you think you are a bit of a Puritan in this respect, make an effort to re-educate yourself. Enjoy the company of people with whom you have a working relationship and if they happen to be particularly admirable or stimulating, then count yourself fortunate. So much depends on your attitude. If you think of business socializing as a chore, that's what it will become, and instead of being an enriching, pleasurable complement to your work, it will be yet another task you don't have time for or get through with gritted teeth.

Managing stress

There's another danger you run if you allow yourself to become seriously overstretched and that is to become a victim of burn-out, one of the most dreaded diseases of modern working life. It happens when people allow themselves to reach a peak of stress from which they can no longer climb down. They get into a cycle of believing that unless they can show how hard they are working they are worthless, until they become so exhausted that they can't relax in the few leisure hours that remain to them.

Burn-out is a devastating experience and in some cases may require professional help. It can cripple you in both your personal and your working life. The symptoms vary from boredom to depression, listlessness or a terrifying feeling that you can no longer cope with any of the stresses in your life. Yet stress in moderation is a healthy and necessary factor in our lives. It keeps us on our toes and makes us ready to meet the challenges, physical or mental, we all need to keep us alive. But each of us has a different stress level and it's important to gauge exactly how much you, the individual, can stand. If it's taking all your energy to tread water, then you can be sure that you have gone over your limit and must pull back immediately.

Start by analysing your week. Go back to those diagrams you filled in with your weekly work and play schedule in chapter 1 and see what's gone wrong. Has it just been an exceptionally busy time recently and can you expect a reprieve shortly, in which case are you prepared to carry on at the same pace for a limited period? Or have you somehow got your schedule out of kilter?

Is there an unresolved problem between balancing your work and home life? This involves politics. If you are a wife and mother you may have to sit down with your husband and children and tell them frankly that you are carrying too many of the domestic burdens. It's a case of negotiating and making known your needs as you would do in any business situation, and if what you need is more help from them, say so frankly. You will feel better for having cleared the air, and they, for their part, are not going to hesitate to let you know what their demands are. As with any negotiation there should be compromise on both sides. Innovation, flexibility and a willingness to make changes are vital in juggling the demands of family and work. Whatever you do, don't let the daily grind of running a household stop you from enjoying your family: delegate the routine work as you would at the office.

Flexibility is the key. It may be that at a certain stage in your career the merging of your personal and business life is quite inevitable. Women, perhaps more than men, are inclined to think that blending their 'private time' with work-related social engagements means sacrificing their personal lives, but this is *not* an either/or situation. You are free to decline or accept as you wish. If you happen to have children of the same age as a close associate you might plan a few outings together that would give you time for your family, and at the same time help to cement a growing friendship. There are good reasons also for keeping a friendly distance in certain business relationships so if you don't care to spend too much time in the evenings and over weekends on business socializing, allocate other time during the working week. But don't then think of it as 'a waste of time'.

In any career there are bound to be times when free evenings or your private social life are curtailed by long hours of work, participation in business-related activities or community organizations. At these times a positive attitude and genuine enjoyment in your work will keep you going. We could all write books on what's wrong with our lives but we tend to short-change each other when it comes to expressing positive feelings. The old maxim to 'count your blessings' is a wise one and it helps to put your complaints and problems into perspective. You will probably find that what has been gnawing away at you isn't nearly as important as it seemed – and certainly not worth spending a lot of time worrying over.

Don't forget the practical steps outlined in chapter 4 to help you make the load easier for yourself: delegation at work and at home; building up a network of supportive business contacts; and consolidating your personal support system.

Advancement by your own design is full of trials and tribulations but it's also fun. It wouldn't be worth doing otherwise so resolve to enjoy it and remember that the choices you make along the way should be yours and yours alone.

The worksheet that concludes this chapter is designed to help you develop a profile of yourself and your wants. It's a good exercise to review these questions on a regular basis – say, every six months. If your answers reflect a serious split between your needs and your current situation, what can you do to close the gap? Check the worksheets that you filled out in chapter 4. Have you begun to take the practical steps necessary to making all areas of your life fulfilling and enjoyable?

WORKSHEET 6

What Do *You* Want?

1. Answer 'yes' or 'no' to the following statements as they relate to you.

   I want to spend more time with my husband/partner

   I want to spend more time with my family

   I want to spend more time with my friends

   I want to reserve my evenings during the week for leisure or family activities rather than work

   I want to reserve my weekends for leisure or family activities

If you answered 'no' to the above questions, you are probably doing a good job of balancing your work and personal life. If you answered 'yes', then there may be is a conflict of some kind. Answer the following questions:

2. Is this conflict temporary or long-term?

3. Can you live with it? For how long?

4. If you can't live with it, what are the steps you can take to resolve it, and by what date?

Step One: Date:

Step Two: Date:

Step Three: Date:

Summary

* Keep your eye on the larger picture
* Take a close look at how you fit into your company's plans and politics
* Be positive about everything – your work and your home life
* Be flexible and open to change and innovation

7

Broadening the Path:
Further Education

'If you don't know where you are going, you will probably end up somewhere else.' – *Laurence J. Peter*

In the last chapter we considered certain important influences on advancement: an ability to perceive the larger picture and exercise political judgement while not forgetting to enjoy yourself are essential elements, and absorbing them into your repertoire will give you a strong handle on the here and now. But planning for the longer term means investing in your future, and one way to achieve this is by undertaking some training or further education.

Women have traditionally been eager to learn and assimilate new information, but they have not always been so adept at learning the political strategy to get the training that is right for them. Each boss, each company and each industry has a different philosophy of learning. You have to make a conscious effort to understand those philosophies and balance them with one based on your own needs. The cost of leaving it to chance can be too high.

Very often companies offer training courses that serve primarily as band-aids. Their people need 'fixing' in certain areas that will add to their immediate short-term usefulness to the company. For example, your company might offer a speed reading course to help you get through massive amounts of documentation. This is very useful to you in your present job and is certainly not to be sneezed at, but you can't look on it as part of your longer-term groundwork for advancement.

Ask around to find out what kind of training your company offers and to whom. Some organizations, notably the clearing banks and a few other forward-thinking companies which pride themselves on their equal-opportunities policies, now issue every member of staff with pamphlets describing in precise detail their training programmes and other facilities for career advancement. There is also Section 56 of the Sex Discrimination Act, which makes a specific provision for single-sex training where it can be shown that women, or men, have not in the past twelve months been given an opportunity to learn a particular skill which would be advantageous to them and their company.

Ask yourself whether you have perhaps been too diffident about putting your name down for a training course. 'The women don't come forward' is a familiar excuse from lazy or chauvinistic managers. Don't give them the opportunity in your case.

It's also sensible to take note of what the people on the fast track in your organization are doing. Which conferences are they attending? Which types of training do they go for? And are they getting their company to sponsor the fees? If you intend learning on the company's territory, three factors will have to be resolved:

1. How to plan your training programme
2. How to pay for it
3. When to study for it

Planning your training programme

Where you start inside a company depends largely on what kind of training or qualifications you have brought to it. Your age and experience also determine the level of training you are likely to be offered, at least at the beginning. Here are a few examples to show what we mean.

If you start with 'O' levels or less, then you will probably be an office clerk and learn general on-the-job office duties like filing, answering the telephone, opening and distributing the mail. Don't despise any of this: it's a basic training which will stand you in good stead for the rest of your working life and will give you a useful insight into the way the company is run. A step up the ladder and you may be a trained secretary but have no experience of using a word processor, so probably the first thing you will need is a rapid induction course to acquaint you with your green-eyed monster. Or you may be an arts graduate who has been accepted for a management training programme which starts with three-month spells in each department lasting for eighteen months, at the end of which time you will be assigned to an area, marketing, for example, where you will develop your career. Possibly you are a graduate who has taken a professional qualification in, say, law or accountancy and you are now completing your articles with a firm where you hope you will be asked to stay on. Or you could be someone who doesn't have many formal qualifications but now that you have gained some useful work experience and have decided which career you wish to pursue, you want to gain some specific qualifications in that area to give you more clout when you apply for your next promotion.

These examples show that not only do your training needs depend on where you start on the ladder, but also that they will change as you progress. At whatever level people begin they must always expect to go through a period of orientation where they may have to learn quite simple, basic skills to enable them to perform specific tasks. This is first-stage training. The second stage is when you identify certain deficiencies in your performance which suggest that you need probably quite a short, concentrated course in a specific area to get it up to scratch. For instance, one person might be given a course in time management because they have poor organizational skills. Another might be given a leadership course to help develop interpersonal skills. Depending upon the number of people requiring specific kinds of help, and on a given organization's particular approach to training, courses such as these may be offered within the office or outside it. Many training consultants will devise tailor-made programmes for different companies, according to their needs, and run the courses in-house.

It is your boss who usually focuses on your current level of performance. This is a good beginning and you should take advantage of all the opportunities that are given to you.

Take the example of Beverley, who started work as a receptionist. She had a naturally easy, pleasant manner and was very good at welcoming people in reception and talking to them on the telephone. Recognizing her potential, her boss offered her the chance to do a training course in telephone sales. At first she felt this training was unnecessary but she agreed to go. The course proved to be excellent: not only did it reinforce her existing style, it also introduced her to sales techniques which she had never imagined would interest her. To her surprise she found that she enjoyed the challenge. Beverley's success on the course led to a promotion into customer services, and now, three years later, she is head of the department.

Once you are in a position to see the whole company picture, it's a good idea to look at possibilities several years down the road and try to anticipate what your company might need. Identify trends and assess the direction in which the company is moving; then educate yourself accordingly.

For instance, we can't stress too strongly how important it is that women should educate themselves in the areas of computers and strategic planning, both of which will be extremely important for advancement in the future. A person should seek this training only after she has had adequate managerial experience, particularly in the area of short- and long-term planning. Women will really have to push to get this kind of 'big picture' training. For one thing, it's very expensive, so your company must feel confident that it's worth investing in you on a long-term basis.

Your training needs depend, as we have seen, on your status in the organization, your boss's expectations for you and where you eventually plan to go. This is where your political judgement plays a useful role. It will help you pinpoint the programmes that are most beneficial to your career. For instance, given what you now know about the first and second stages of training, it is politically wise to request a shift from training which focuses on narrow, task-related skills to courses with a broader range. For example, learning about supervision, budget planning, team building and so on is to be acquiring the skills you need to prepare you for a leadership role. Consider in this context as well courses that teach you about public speaking and how to run effective meetings (more about these essential skills later in this chapter).

If your organization isn't very forthcoming about the kind of training it offers, and to whom, have no hesitation in approaching someone in the personnel department – it's their job to be accessible to employees – and ask them the following questions:

1. What are the accepted training policies and practices for someone at your level?

2. Which courses does your organization see as beneficial to its needs?

3. Which courses does your organization pay for?

4. Who are you likely to meet by attending certain programmes?

Training programmes can take three basic forms:

1. Degrees, certificates or diplomas

2. In-house seminars and courses

3. Workshops and conferences

Each of these has its advantages and disadvantages. Don't limit yourself to only one: there's a time and a place for all of them.

Degrees, certificates or diplomas
The range of business studies courses at polytechnics, universities, some colleges of higher education and business schools is now very extensive. The great advantage of a formal learning programme lasting for two, three, possibly more years, is that the learning units follow a careful plan. They progress from simple to more complex material in an orderly fashion and these modules are designed to complement and build on each other. A good degree course, in particular, will teach you more than just the subject matter it encompasses; it will help you develop your abstract reasoning powers and teach you how to analyse and

solve problems. That ability, as we pointed out in chapter 6, will stand you in good stead throughout your career.

Obtaining a formal degree or diploma has a certain cachet and there is no doubt that your academic success will increase your general self-confidence but, do be warned: a degree or other similar piece of paper only provides an entry point in the marketplace. It does not guarantee automatic advancement, nor does it teach you any of the necessary survival skills. While people with degrees may have a certain edge when it comes to getting that first job, there are no studies indicating that in the long term the formally educated advance further than those with fewer academic credentials.

Another potential disadvantage of studying for a degree is that it takes a long time. If you can only do a part-time night course it may take you five to ten years to get that precious piece of paper. It really depends what you are studying. If it is for some kind of additional professional qualification to be, say, an accountant, banker or company secretary – all professions which demand certain examinations before allowing you to advance – then you have no choice. But if the value of the degree you have chosen is somewhat dubious, at least in relation to your chosen career, you may end up spending an inordinate amount of time, money and energy without achieving great results.

Consider these two stories. Grace had a first degree in French and German and taught these languages for many years in a mixed comprehensive. She improved her academic qualifications, first with a Masters which took her two years of part-time study and then with a Ph.D which took several years more culminating in a year's sabbatical. She had just been promoted to head of the language department before the sabbatical but had to resign as the school couldn't run its large 'O' and 'A' level classes without an active head. Grace took the risk because she felt that this step would cause only a minor hiccup in her progress towards her ultimate goal – acquiring a school headship. Alas, her judgement proved wrong. She couldn't get back to her previous position and she was turned down on several applications for deputy headships in other parts of the country. Even with her formal degrees, she was not considered a serious candidate beacuse she lacked the key administrative experience required for the job. She had overestimated the value of formal qualifications and underestimated the role of experience and direct preparation for the job.

Pauline, on the other hand, had a much more realistic expectation of what she wanted from her MBA (Masters in Business Administration). Her first degree was in History and she had worked for ten years with various academic publishers, rising to the position of senior editor. Although she enjoyed the work, she realized that she was never going to progress very far because the field was too specialized, so she decided that she would equip herself to start an entirely new career in the commercial sector. She arranged a loan to pay for an intensive, one-year MBA programme at a leading business school, beat her brains out over subjects she thought she could never tackle, like statistics, but found herself hugely stimulated by the challenge, and today, seven years later, is heading up the marketing division of a major financial services firm in the City.

Before you rush to commit yourself to years of study, you should carry out the following research:

1. Visit the library or student services centre at your local college or university and read up on the courses which interest you. Even better, go directly to the department or faculty in which you want to study and talk to professors or student advisers there. Ask them to explain the full range of options in the various courses and the final degree or diplomas offered.

2. Speak to at least three graduates from the programme which you intend to do and ask them, among other things, what they consider to have been the long-term value for them of following that particular course of study.

3. Discuss this information with your current employer (or another appropriate adviser if you are planning to do the course as a stepping stone out of your present company), and explore whether the course really would be beneficial to your future career.

One last point about academic training: some people thrive in a formal classroom situation; others don't. You may feel more comfortable on an in-house programme or a workshop, where students tend to participate more and are often encouraged to get hands-on experience. Some skills and technical knowledge are only available at academic institutions, but, wherever possible, choose the system that you feel best suits your style.

In-house seminars and courses

Many organizations offer a variety of training opportunities for their staff, many of them sponsored by the company. Never turn down an invitation to attend these courses, and go a bit further: if you see an external course advertised which you think would be really helpful to you, ask the right person in authority to sponsor you.

Here are some reasons why you should take these initiatives:

1. In-house courses are used by companies to develop skills which their management feel will satisfy their practical needs.

2. Organizations design programmes that fit their culture, their philosophy and the directions in which they are headed.

3. People with potential for advancement are often identified in these programmes.

4. Not only do these programmes improve your skills and enhance your visibility, they are also often a source of support groups.

Christine is a young employee with a very progressive retail chain of shops which provides management training for staff who are being considered for store managers. She went through a one-month management training programme, and during her course she became friends with Doris, a senior store manager who conducted some of the company seminars. When Christine completed her programme she received her assignment in a small town, a post that did not really attract her, but nevertheless she took it gracefully and performed well. Six months later Doris had an opening in her store and requested that Christine be transferred to her location.

The point of this story is that Christine's training programme equipped her not only with new learning but also with useful contacts within her organization; this is a major advantage of in-house programmes. These relationships last because they live on in the organizational environment and often this bonding gives women some valuable support in the course of their careers, support they may need more than a piece of paper.

Remember, however, that in some cases companies will offer courses that serve their own interests rather than those of their employees. While their political benefits can be as useful as they were in Christine's case, you may still have to go outside the company for serious training with long-term value. Always look carefully at each course on offer and assess its potential benefits for you.

Workshops and conferences

There are innumerable opportunities for learning in public workshops or seminars (see Resources on pages 219–226 for some recommended training organizations). Their variety gives you a chance to select ones which are not merely useful to your present employer but can also provide you with some of the basic groundwork you need to develop your career. Another attraction of these gatherings is that you are exposed to fresh ideas and information coming from participants who work in other companies, possibly even in quite different industries.

There is, however, a temptation you should resist: flitting from one workshop to another on impulse instead of working out where they belong in your larger plan. There are so many available, with exciting agendas and usually lasting no longer than a day or two, but, unlike academic courses, they do not necessarily complement each other or add up to a comprehensive grounding in areas that interest you.

The workshops that are of inestimable value are those which are sponsored by your particular industry and run by key people who have a great deal of expertise on specific topics. Studying with them will increase your skills and enhance your visibility as well as giving you a chance to network with people outside your organization.

Who pays for your advanced training?

Company policies concerning payment or other help for further formal training vary quite considerably. If you need the qualifications to move up the management structure – for instance, doing the Institute of Banking exams is necessary for all aspiring bank managers – then you will be allowed to do some of your learning in company time. Other organizations may be open to negotiation, particularly if you can show that the proposed course is relevant to your work. At the very least, a company may agree to keep your job open if you want to take a year off, say, to do an MBA.

It's sensible to open up a discussion with your employers before you sign up for any course to see just what they are prepared to do for you. Come to the discussion well prepared, showing how the course will improve your skills and future contribution.

An important thing to remember about formal degrees is that most of the learning involved will be done in your own time. Even if your company agrees to let you have some part-time day-release to attend lectures, you will still have to do your studying – reading and writing essays – in your own spare time. In that sense, academic courses require a considerable personal investment of your time and commitment, irrespective of whether you pay for them.

Sometimes, people who want to pursue formal training will do so only if their company agrees to pick up the tab. It may be that their self-esteem is threatened by a corporate refusal to finance education; on the other hand, the company may only be carrying out what is long-established company policy to which no exceptions are made. Forget about imagined insults to your pride. If you know that the course will make an important difference to your career, refusing to pay for it yourself represents a 'penny-wise, pound-foolish' planning strategy which you are bound to regret later. The company's refusal possibly indicates the low value they put on this qualification, but they may be wrong and you be right. Who says that you have got to stay with that company for the rest of your working life? Look around you and you may observe that many of the men and women who have moved most rapidly through their organizations are self-starters and 'self-payers'. They have been able to balance their long-term gains with the short-term burdens of paying for training they know they need. Never give up at the first setback. It has even been known for friendly bank managers to grant loans at a special low-interest rate.

As far as sponsorship for outside workshops and conferences is concerned, company policies vary from generous to non-existent. Fund allocation may vary even within a company, some departments being much better than others, or there may be a clearcut policy on the amount available to each individual which depends on their rank and job. It may be that only a certain number of company representatives are allowed to attend a given conference. Whatever the policy in your organization, find out about the key training decisions it has made and which conferences it supports heavily, because these are the ones it is most likely to pay for.

The following worksheet is designed to help you determine in what areas you need training. You should review your priorities at each step in your climb up the ladder and revise your plan accordingly. Take an active, dynamic approach. What was good last year may not be of any use to you this year. As always, *set goals*.

WORKSHEET 7

Deciding about Training

1. How would you rate your skills in:

	Excellent	Good	Needs improvement
Technical performance of your present job			
Planning			
Problem-solving			
Motivating your subordinates			
Coordinating staff			
Delegating			
Decision-making			
Budget-planning			
Generating profit			
Representing your firm to the public			

2. Do you plan to increase your knowledge in specific areas such as management planning, problem-solving, motivation, coordinating, decision-making?

3. Have you selected programmes that will help you to accomplish personal and career goals, either short- or long-term?

4. If you are already in a training programme, what are the benefits you see it having for you?

Short-term:

Long-term:

5. Is there a mentor or colleague presently giving you emotional support or new information who can steer you towards the right training programme?

6. Is your company willing to pay all or at least part of the cost of your training?

7. If not, are you willing to pay for it?

8. If your training will require study or work in your spare time, are you willing to go ahead with it?

If you are planning a rational, long-term approach to career advancement, then taking a hodgepodge of courses isn't going to be enough. It's obviously necessary to acquire all the specialized technical skills you need for your particular niche in your industry, but you should also plan to include those broader, generalized skills that will prepare you to be a manager.

The temptation to go out and learn is exciting, but also confusing. Select one or two skills you know you need and establish a time frame in which to acquire them so that you don't just attend trendy workshop discussions which have no clear purpose or discernible outcome.

We are concluding this chapter by looking at three areas where women definitely need to improve their skills if they want to move up in business. They are: making presentations, running effective meetings and handling interviews. You must learn to be good at all three activities: feeling shy or pleading lack of confidence are simply not valid excuses once you reach a certain level in your organization. It's a matter of developing your political instincts and not forgetting that there's also a fun element involved. There's the agony, yes, but also there's the ecstasy of pulling off a really successful presentation.

Presentation skills and public speaking

Many women are still very hesitant about speaking up in meetings, be they formal or informal. If you recognize this as a failing in yourself, consider some of the negative side effects it causes. Obviously, it impairs your visibility and limits your opportunities to establish your professional credibility. You let yourself down by failing to assert your professional identity, and you let down your company team by not being an active enough spokeswoman for it in business situations.

A deficiency in public speaking is not merely a potential liability: it is a serious handicap and, if steps are not taken to correct it, it can, quite literally, become a chronic disease. Women who avoid making presentations or speaking in public tend to grow ever more fearful of doing so. If this fear is allowed to continue, the prognosis is dismal. Women who refuse to accept the responsibility and risk of putting themselves squarely in the public eye will never make it to the top.

Diane, for instance, has worked as an office manager for a charitable organization for over eight years. She is a capable administrator and prepares all the financial reports for the audit committee. She has been asked repeatedly by the members of this committee to present her reports to them and to the executive committee. However, she is so paralysed by a fear of public speaking that she refuses even to read the reports. These presentations occur regularly but Diane always calls on the organization's accountant or permits her subordinates to take her place and enjoy the limelight.

Diane, who is technically capable and a very competent manager, is losing ground. Not only is her problem eroding her already low self-esteem, but the organization is finding it such a nuisance that it has confronted Diane and told her frankly that her inhibitions are standing in the way of her advancement.

This problem is even more serious for the woman who is self-employed. She, in particular, must be constantly selling and promoting herself, and effective presentations are an important part of this.

Rowena owns and operates her own travel agency and in the course of her work she is often asked to give talks on tour packages for convention planners. However, she is so terrified of making the presentations that she always brings along a sales representative from the agency who carries it off for her. But there is a price to pay: Rowena's credibility is lessened. People are beginning to wonder if she or her business have the reserves to complete a particular project because she always avoids direct communication.

Both Diane and Rowena must take immediate steps to overcome their problems. Even those who have no qualms about public speaking can have problems of a reverse order. Theresa, for instance, is a top executive with a merchant bank who often attends or chairs meetings with clients. Her heartiness encourages such extreme volubility that assistants who accompany her make a point of announcing another appointment for the time when her meeting is due to end.

Although people like her, she is generally regarded as a bore and a time-waster.

Fortunately, good presentation skills are not confined to those who enjoy showing off or have a natural flair for performing publicly; they can be learned, and each time you practise them you will get better.

Start to develop your confidence by mastering small tasks such as introducing a speaker or delivering a vote of thanks. Watch how other, polished speakers perform and see if you can pick up any tips from them. Try and identify the specifics of your anxiety: is it sweaty hands, a dry throat or an uncontrollably shaky voice? Each of these has a separate remedy which can be mastered.

The best way to tackle your fears is to take a course with one of the many excellent instructors who have developed their own programmes for building confidence and acquiring the skills for preparing and delivering presentations. A course with video guarantees the best results. Seeing yourself on camera is a salutary – if sometimes painful – learning experience.

Here are a few survival tips for public speaking and presentations:

1. Do not just learn your lines by memory. Really concentrate on understanding the concepts and the arguments that you are trying to communicate. Make notes on cards if that helps.

2. Make sure that any visual aids you may be using – for example slides or an overhead projector – are in good functioning order and test them out beforehand.

3. Develop a title for every presentation that you offer and state it emphatically to your audience before starting. This title should reflect your key objective in giving the presentation.

4. Define all your key terms early in the presentation.

5. Be prepared for, but not put off by, members of the audience asking questions early on in your presentation, and don't hesitate to suggest that they would be better answered at the end of the session if that's the way you prefer to handle it.

6. Try to keep any discussion on track and focused.

7. Summarize your major points and present a conclusion which leaves your audience clearly understanding the purpose of your presentation, even if they didn't listen to every word.

8. Be prepared for questions which may lead away from the topic under discussion but still have some relevance. You should also have your own questions ready to help the audience get started if they don't have questions right away.

Running effective meetings

The skills required to run effective meetings involve two major factors:

1. Your own performance as a leader

2. The attitude of your group to meetings

Today more than ever, organizations are involving staff in meetings, committees and task forces to deal with every aspect of organizational life. While meetings can be very productive, many of them are mishandled because of poor preparation, weak leadership and an inability to manage the time spent in them efficiently.

Every organization has one or two managers, like the verbose Theresa, whose meetings are dreaded. The most common complaint is the 'one-hour' staff meeting that drags on for three hours and includes twenty-six items on the agenda. The staff at such meetings become very frustrated because they have scheduled other activities, and some people have to leave the meeting at different times due to other obligations. The agenda is over-extended because no clear priorities have been set, either by the leader or by the group. These meetings are boring and do not provide even a basic communication tool; quite the contrary, they turn people off.

As an executive, your running of a successful meeting will require:

1. A sharp understanding of group processes, communication and decision-making skills

2. A good knowledge of the subjects involved and their rele-

vance to the agenda and the particular decision or decisions that must be made

3. Good observational skills to understand people's positions, vested interests, who are the allies and who the scapegoats

Most important, know your own position and be ready to substantiate it with facts, figures, statistics and summary statements. Bring copies of any reports or statements you may have to consult in the course of the meeting. Even if you are not running the meeting, you should help to ensure that the discussions are clear and that the record in the minutes reflects what was agreed upon.

If you have been asked to chair a meeting, you should carry out the following preparations in advance:

1. Consider whether the meeting is strictly necessary. Possibly a memo, telephone conversation or other style of communication might be more effective.

2. Decide carefully what your objectives for this particular meeting are.

3. Plan your agenda and send it to the key participants ahead of time so that they can prepare their contribution.

4. If the choice of participants at the meeting is up to you, select those people who have real contributions to make.

5. Announce the time and place of the meeting and make sure you reserve the room or area well in advance.

Always get your meetings started on time, and keep the discussion on topic. Otherwise, your whole meeting becomes the 'absent member agenda' which means that you are using up time scheduled for the meeting talking about the people who haven't shown up. To avoid unnecessary hanging about, the chairperson should make it clear that he or she expects apologies in advance from those who will not be able to attend the meeting.

Even if there is a senior executive attending the meeting, try to avoid addressing them throughout the entire session as if you are seeking their approval. It's embarrassing and irritating. Use the whole group's potential, not just the opinion of one person; otherwise, you don't need a meeting.

The best meetings take place when:

1. The chairperson knows the appropriate style for the meeting. This can range from formal to very informal, depending on circumstances or on the organization.

2. The chairperson is a good listener, is not easily sidetracked and speaks only to focus the meeting.

3. The chairperson summarizes decisions and is capable of following through on implementation – who, what, where, when and how.

4. All those in attendance are expected to contribute to the planning, preparation and evaluation of the meeting.

Interviewing skills

Being in the spotlight by, for instance, running effective meetings and giving concise presentations is very important to your visibility. But learning how to handle yourself in interviews is critical to your survival in the workplace. Because of the fierce competition in the marketplace, more and more interviews are being conducted for every position that becomes available. Consequently, your chances of landing a job at first crack are very low. Not only will you be subject to being interviewed by different companies, but once you become a serious candidate for a job, you will probably have several interviews at different levels within the organization. Getting the first interview can be a problem in itself. Here are some pointers:

1. In any telephone contact you make with an organization, always make it your objective to set an interview date and time.

2. Whether you are sending or delivering your curriculum vitae (CV) make sure that it looks impeccable and utterly professional. It should be typed, well laid out and letter-perfect. Keep it as brief and succinct as you can, no more than one side of an A4 page if possible. Highlight the most important functions of your past work that relate to the job you want, and any particularly impressive achievements.

3. Try to bypass the rigid personnel procedures and find out the name of the person directly responsible for hiring and interviewing. Make a direct contact with this person, perhaps by phoning, and be sure that your CV lands on his or her desk.

4. If you are interested in joining a particular company, ask around to find out who is responsible for hiring and, even if no job has been advertised, write directly to that person, explaining your interest and enclosing your CV. Follow this up with a telephone call to try to arrange a meeting.

The critical test of whether or not you will be hired depends on how you handle interview situations and the face-to-face opportunities they provide. We use the positive word 'opportunities' because people become so anxious about interviews that they tend to see them as a battle ground. Courses in job searching are now common and most of them deal with interview skills. Here are a few brief tips to help you prepare yourself:

1. Your self-presentation should be appropriate to the industry you want to be in. If you are looking for a job in 'creative' fields, such as advertising or the fashion industry, you have more scope with regard to what you wear. You don't need to fear bright colours or the latest style as long as you don't overdo it. But most other industries – banks and insurance companies, for instance, or indeed any company where there is a preponderance of men – tend to be conservative, and you should dress accordingly.

2. Develop a vocabulary that makes you sound as if you know what you are talking about without sounding pretentious. If you have proven organizational and decision-making abilities, then say so. Similarly, any specialized experience with budgets, financial statements and computers must be emphasized, and do it all in such a manner that it's clear you have highly developed interpersonal skills. It may help to practise with a friend before you go to the actual interview.

3. Pull out what is unique about yourself or the services you can offer. Why should a company choose you over hundreds of other

applicants? Blow your own trumpet – truthfully and without making your interviewer deaf!

4. Always do some research on the company or organization that has offered you the interview. Look at the last three Annual Reports and make enquiries of any friends who may have information. Look the company up in the reference section of your local library and make a point of reading your newspaper's business pages regularly so that you keep in touch with company developments. Preliminary research serves two basic purposes. First, it shows that you have done your homework, and are therefore committed and interested; second, it identifies you as resourceful and alert.

5. Have your questions ready about the compensation package, including health and other fringe benefits, but keep them for the final interview.

6. Ask when they would like you to start work and be firm about the notice obligations you may have to work out for your current employer. This shows that you are positive, confident and practical, as well as fair.

Carol is a psychologist who had worked for fifteen years in one hospital. When she wanted to change her position to a new setting, she resolved that she would go anywhere in the country and that she was open to offers outside the NHS. One of her ideas was that she would like to join a private career counselling service. She was surprised and dismayed by the difficulties she encountered in getting even to first base – the job interview – despite sending out dozens of CVs and letters.

Sensibly, she decided she could do with a few practical tips so she joined up for a course on interviewing techniques. The most important new practice she learned was to get an interview appointment on the telephone while discussing the posting of her CV. Having mastered the art of obtaining interviews, she then learnt how to find out about other openings on the grapevine. It took her more than six months to get a job, and there were many rejections along the way, but in the end she got exactly what she wanted. She is a senior counsellor in a reputable vocational guidance organization and you can be sure she is passing on her new-found skills to her clients. She actually got her new job after being referred by one person to a colleague in another organization where he knew they were looking for just such a person as Carol.

The point in Carol's case is that she didn't allow her initial fear of interviews to hold her back. She forced herself to keep going and to acquire new skills. Each interview was a learning experience in itself and now she has not only an enjoyable new job but also renewed confidence in her ability to overcome obstacles and handle unfamiliar situations.

One final point: whether or not you are looking for a new job, it's a good idea to go to one or two interviews a year. This keeps you abreast of other opportunities in your business and it brushes up your interviewing techniques so that when you do go after a job you really want, you will feel much more at ease.

Courses in all these subjects are available through company training programmes and in management workshops and seminars run by private consultants. (Consult Resources for names of good ones.)

Meanwhile fill out the following worksheet to review your present training wants and needs. Be as specific as possible in identifying the skills you would like to acquire.

WORKSHEET 8

Advanced Training

WITHIN YOUR ORGANIZATION

1. What opportunities exist for training?

2. How are people selected for it?

3. What is offered?

4. What specific interests or skills requiring training has your boss identified as being useful to you? To your department?

5. What programmes have you been assigned to attend?

6. What specific set of interests have you identified to your boss?

7. What programmes have you jointly selected?

1. Referring to the table on page 130, what are the skills you have identified as being of potential interest to you (rank them in order of priority)?

2. Have you investigated possible training programmes for acquiring these skills?

3. Have you presented these possibilities to your organization and found out if it is willing to help with payment of fees or time off?

4. Have you set a date or dates by which you want to complete various steps in your training? If not, set them now.

5. Have you allocated time in which to study or attend classes? How much time do you estimate you will need on a weekly basis?

6. Have you adjusted your personal support system to accommodate the time you must spend on training (e.g., babysitting, grocery shopping, etc.)?

Summary

* Identify specific areas of training that will benefit your career, both now and in the future

* Choose the programme that's right for you

* Find out what help your organization is prepared to give you

* Sharpen your skills in: making presentations
                                                           running effective meetings
                                                             handling interviews

8

Negotiation:
the Skill You Can Take Everywhere

Negotiation is commonly associated with big business and political life. This is misleading because it blurs our understanding of a force that has a profound influence on the internal workings of organizations and people of all kinds at all levels. Whether at home, at work, at school or in an association, any woman who interacts with other people will, over a period of time, find herself grappling with the intricacies of negotiation.

Every time you plan to go to the theatre with a group of friends, for instance, and you talk about which play each of you wants to see, you are negotiating. Each person's tastes, interests and the amount of money they want to spend are subject to discussion. The same is true when you and your family discuss which household tasks are to be performed by whom, or where you will go on your next holiday.

You can discover a lot about your general weaknesses and strengths by examining your own way of dealing with these personal negotiations. Do you assert your own wants and needs when you discuss issues with your family, or do you tend, as many women do, to give in 'because their needs are greater than mine' and it just doesn't seem that important? Do you become emotional and express possibilities as demands or ultimatums, or can you keep your cool? Are you open to suggestions you hadn't considered before? Are you willing to make trade-offs and compromises, and is your family or group of friends willing to do the same? Do you feel that people are constantly taking advantage of you?

As you can see, negotiation affects every sphere of life, including your work. Anyone, therefore, who is, or aspires to be, in a managerial position should have a basic understanding of the process of negotiation. Superficially, it appears very simple. To negotiate, the dictionary tells us, is 'to talk over and arrange terms'. But negotiation can be much more complex and long-lasting than you might expect. Nothing could be simpler in definition but broader in scope than negotiation.

It is particularly necessary for women to develop their negotiating skills in the workplace because they start at a serious disadvantage. It is well known that in spite of the legislation and even the recent amendments to the Equal Pay Act following a directive from the European Parliament, there are still discrepancies in pay between men and women with comparable experience doing work of equal value. Improving your negotiating skills is one way of making sure that you don't fall prey to this kind of subtle discrimination.

Fill out the following worksheet as objectively and specifically as you can. If you do not have any experience in business negotiations, draw on your memories of personal negotiations with friends or family. Be as critical as possible in identifying your own strengths and weaknesses.

WORKSHEET 9

Your Experience in Negotiation

1. Looking back at successful negotiations, what do you feel were your three main strengths (e.g., persuasiveness, well-prepared arguments, political judgement, timing etc.)?

    i.

    ii.

    iii.

2. Did you exploit these strengths to their greatest advantage, or were you 'lucky'?

3. What are the three main weaknesses you see in your performance as a negotiator (e.g., difficulty in expressing your arguments, letting your emotions take over, unwillingness to compromise, etc.)?

    i.

    ii.

    iii.

4. Is there a recurring negative pattern in your negotiating style (e.g., when you feel you're losing you can't retain your composure)?

    i.

    ii.

    iii.

5. Are there particular subjects you find difficult to discuss in negotiations (e.g., salary, working conditions, responsibilities, etc.)?

    i.

    ii.

    iii.

6. Do you feel intimidated when negotiating with someone in a position of higher authority than yourself?

7. Examine some specific unsuccessful negotiations you have experienced. Can you think of arguments you could have made – or ways in which you could have made them – that might have turned the situation around? What would you do now if you could start the negotiation(s) over again?

8. What skills do you think you need to work on in order to succeed in future negotiations?

    i.

    ii.

    iii.

In today's complex world, negotiations take place all the time. For instance, one member of a department will have to meet deadlines set by salespeople who may want to change them at short notice. If you are trying to get information into or out of the corporate computer, you may need to negotiate for computer time. If you are trying to book a service for a client you may have to negotiate special terms. If you are a university student who can't produce an essay on time, you may attempt to negotiate an extension with your tutor.

Every culture handles negotiations differently; so for that matter, does every industry. We have included some useful texts on negotiation in Further Reading and they will help you to understand which particular techniques might be appropriate in your own situation. Some of them will help you to understand the importance of non-verbal communication strategies, others will explain the specifics involved in negotiating anything from a car loan to a promotion. When selecting books, check through their introductions to see if they provide the general information you are seeking or, if it's something quite specific you want – like how to conduct salary negotiations – then choose one that focuses on that subject.

You may also want to investigate courses on negotiating skills. They are available at any college running an industrial relations course, through your trade union, or the Industrial Society, or other private management consultancies.

Six survival tips for negotiating

When you arrive at the corporate negotiating table, make sure that you are mentally prepared and physically fully alert. Questions you should ask yourself, and answer beforehand, include the following: Do you know the precedents, the existing laws or company policies on the issue you intend to discuss? What have been the results of previous negotiations, both in your own experience and in that of your colleagues?

Suppose, for instance, that you want a two-month leave of absence without pay. Have you found out whether other people in your department have ever been granted a similar leave? Have certain people been refused and others permitted to go? Does your reason for wanting this leave tie in with a corporate objective? You need this kind of information to get a good grasp of the issue *before* you begin to negotiate. You will also have to consider other factors such as timing. Are you initiating a negotiation with your boss at a time when you are both under pressure?

The following is a list of the most essential survival skills you must bring to any business negotiation:

1. Reviewing and refining your objectives
2. Understanding the other side's negotiating plan
3. Knowing the buzz words
4. Developing a positive attitude and climate for discussion
5. Sending the right messages
6. Using your powers of observation

1. *Reviewing and refining objectives*

Defining what you want to happen in a negotiation is the first step you should take, but you must accept that you won't always get exactly what you want. So always come to the negotiating table armed with a contingency plan. In short, you must know what you are prepared to accept in lieu of what you want.

If, for instance, you are buying a word processor, you may want not only the equipment itself at the lowest possible price but also free delivery, a good service warranty and the right instalment-payment plan. In the course of buying the word processor you will probably find that you can't get all these extras; for example, you may have to forego free delivery in order to get a lower price. Decide which of these advantages is most important to you – an extended payment period may be more helpful than a rock-bottom price – and negotiate accordingly. Your last resort, obviously, is to pay full price for the word processor without achieving any of these concessions. You could, in such circumstances, say that your negotiation has failed.

If this is true of a buying situation where you are usually in a strong position, imagine what a difference it makes to be a

149

shrewd negotiator when you are asking for something of special benefit to you, say a salary increase. As the scouts say, *be prepared*.

2. *Understanding the other side's negotiating plan*

Experienced negotiators have many tactics and many alternative plans up their sleeves. They often work as teams with strategems which they have carefully worked out in advance. In the fashion industry, for instance, two buyers will visit a supplier at the end of the season to buy clearances. During the meeting, one buyer may excuse herself and take the time to check the inventory levels in the warehouse. If they are high, the buyers know that the supplier has excess stock and will be open to accepting a lower price. A clever supplier, on the other hand, will anticipate this ruse and rearrange his or her inventory accordingly.

The more each side in a negotiation knows, or guesses, about the other's strategy, the more complex and sophisticated the negotiation becomes. In attempting to assess your negotiating situation, you should pay attention to all the following: pay-offs, time lags, contingency plans, closing and implementation.

i. *Pay-offs*

People will often try to distract you from the real matter under discussion by bringing up side issues that have less significance for them. They do this to make you feel that they are making a concession even though it isn't one. Later on, they may become very tough about an issue – or *the* issue – of great importance to you. So watch for signs early on in the process of a negotiation that indicate where the other side's real interests or intentions lie.

What matters in negotiations is an understanding of the bottom line, both your own and your 'opponent's'. At what point is the deal still attractive to the other party? At what point will they walk away, leaving you with nothing to negotiate?

ii. *Time lags*

Be aware when others are using time delays simply to confuse or stall negotiations. Good timing on your part is also absolutely essential.

People will adjust their scheduling to make you anxious.

Stalling is only good if you are sure that the other person has fewer options than you have. If, for instance, you are buying a new home, you may want to stall a bit in order to bring down the seller's asking price or give you time to find a buyer for your own property. But this strategy only works if you are quite sure that the seller has not already received offers more attractive than your own. Should that be the case, you risk losing the opportunity to make any firm offer at all so tread with care when stalling. If the other side stalls, analyse their motives and ask yourself whether you think their action is justified.

Adjournments are often used by negotiators to reorganize their strategies. You can stop a negotiation in order to reassess your position or collect new information – and so can the other side.

iii. *Contingency plans*
Prepare your own contingency plans and alternatives thoroughly and, as far as possible, imagine what the other side's alternative options are likely to be. Providing you have pre-established in your own mind the objectives on which you are prepared to come to an agreement, you will be less likely to be thrown off your guard by an unexpected suggestion during the negotiation, possibly causing you to agree to something you later regret. Try to foresee all the possible arguments that will be raised to counter your objectives, and prepare your own counter-arguments.

iv. *Closing*
Every negotiation has a conclusion. Decide in advance how you want to seal the deal. Depending on the circumstances, this may take the form of a formal contract, a signed memo, a payment of money or even a handshake. If you can convince the other side that their requirements have been met, and you respond to their arguments positively and unambiguously, they will be ready to close the negotiation.

v. *Implementation*
Establish guidelines for agreement, follow-ups and implementation of the terms to which you have agreed. Let's take

the example we used earlier – buying a word processor. If one of your conditions in so doing is to have a complementary training session to learn to use the equipment, you should ensure that this requirement is spelt out in the sales contract. The same principle applies to work negotiations. If you are being offered a training course, a rise or a bigger departmental budget, make sure that you have agreed on dates and the ways in which the changes will be effected.

3. *Knowing the buzz words*
Once you start to get involved in negotiating for your company you will find that people use a lot of jargon. This serves a useful purpose as a shorthand for complex processes which, if they had to be spelt out each time, would make the whole negotiation very long and drawn out, so become familiar with it.

Many of us work today in industries that are very specialized with their own particular buzz words and abbreviations. We drop names easily and expect the other party to know whom or what we are talking about, but, if they don't, they may misunderstand you or their ignorance can make them feel insecure and defensive which could have a bad effect on the ultimate outcome of the discussion. Arrange to hold a brief clarification session at the beginning of the negotiation so that both sides can explain any specialist words or acronyms they intend using.

4. *Developing a positive attitude and climate for discussion*
One of the major purposes of negotiating is to convince the other party that they have something to gain from the discussion, even if you are the one asking for something. Consequently, it's important to establish an atmosphere of mutual trust and respect.

Take Anthea, for example, who specializes in training young women managers working in hotels and catering, not an industry noted for its generosity towards its employees. Anthea has made it her business to be thoroughly clued-up on all the government grants that are now available to employers, so when she presents her training package to her prospective clients she has written into it the various allowances that can be claimed. The clients are grateful because Antheas's foresight has saved them money and this predisposes them to accepting her services.

Try to be as constructive as possible in all your negotiations. To start off by threatening or making angry demands is to court disaster. Brenda Dean, General Secretary of Sogat 82, who led her union through an exceptionally difficult year in its dispute with News International, won praise on all sides for her calm, firm but always charming manner. Incidentally, she said that far worse than the endless sleepless nights spent in fruitless argument was the unfailing diet of beer and sandwiches.

You should never be afraid of stating your position and your reasons for taking it, but, at the same time, be positive and open when listening to what the other side has to say. Negotiations don't have to be confrontational. Women are, on the whole, more inclined to be cooperative than men; we should be using this trait positively and to our advantage in all our negotiations, without, of course, taking conciliation to the point of giving in. Whenever possible, contribute any information that will help the other side arrive at a satisfying solution to their problem, just so long as it doesn't leave you at a disadvantage.

5. *Sending the right messages*

Personal style is both verbal and non-verbal. Clear communication is obviously vital but, in addition to making your language unambiguous, have you also examined your self-presentation and have you considered how it might be interpreted by others? Even when you are not talking, you should make sure that your listening attitudes, expressions, body language and display of interest are all consistent with the message you want to deliver. For instance, no matter how strong your arguments, what will the other party in a negotiation think if you refuse to look them in the eye, shift constantly in your seat, look at your watch as if you were late for another appointment or cover your mouth every time you speak?

If you think you are letting yourself down in this respect, it might be a good idea to do a course in assertiveness-training or self-presentation (or both). Alternatively, if it's just for a one-off occasion and you haven't got time to enrol on a course before, say, asking your boss for a rise, you could do a role play with a good friend who can comment on your body language.

6. *Using your powers of observation*

Your observational skills will help you assess the other side's non-verbal behaviour while you are listening to what they have to say. For instance, is the other party's body language attacking or defensive? Often you can tell whether someone is going to be difficult just by the way they enter the room and don't greet you. Be prepared to have to work at bringing them to your way of thinking.

It's extraordinary how revealing body language is, once you have trained yourself to interpret the many and varied gestures that people make, often quite unwittingly. If your opponents feel they are winning, for instance, they may start to grin, their teeth bared but their eyes cold and hard. Or if they feel defeat impending, they may show it by frowning, chewing their nails, playing with their hair or exhibiting other nervous mannerisms. It's said that you can't trust a person who strokes their nose – it means they're telling you a lie. For an amusing but instructive compendium of unconscious human behaviour read Desmond Morris's book, *Manwatching*.

Apart from body language, the other party may exhibit behaviour of which you should take careful note. Threats, name-calling, bragging and other kinds of provocative behaviour are often used by negotiators who are not sufficiently confident or skilled to create a positive climate. If you are negotiating with a team, one person may play the part of tough guy, the other that of the soft touch. It is crucial that these tactics be identified for what they are, and are not taken personally. Keep your cool.

As we pointed out earlier, bargaining and counterproposals can be introduced as ways of bringing in new options – or as red herrings to obscure the real issue. Watch carefully. Is a particular subject being raised inappropriately? Are certain ideas either being rushed through or ignored? Without being either antagonistic or accusatory, try to steer the negotiation back to what you consider relevant.

Finally, be aware that 'selective perception' can work for and against you. Not everyone will hear everything you say. What they do hear, they may interpret differently from your original intention. People's body language or words in response to your arguments may indicate that you have been misunderstood. Monitor them to make sure that you are communicating effectively.

Advance preparation, the ability to size up a situation quickly, and keen powers of observation provide the foundations upon which sound negotiating skills are based. You can begin to hone these abilities by consciously exercising them in everyday situations; also try to attend negotiations at which you are an observer rather than a participant. This removes the anxiety and strong emotions you may experience when playing an active part in negotiating. And if the negotiation involves your colleagues, you will have a good idea of their style and strategies before you negotiate with them yourself.

Once you have had this experience of watching a negotiation in full spate, answer the questions in the following worksheet.

WORKSHEET 10

Observing Negotiations

1. Is this a team negotiation or a one-to-one?

2. Who are the participants? Is there a chairperson?

3. Is there a statement of purpose or of specific objectives?

4. Advance preparations. Note how much information has been consolidated in letters, memos, files, technical and legal preparation.

5. Are presentations formal or informal?

6. Observe the participants. What does their behaviour reveal about the following:

	Participant 1	Participant 2
Interest		
Expertise		
Attitude (positive or negative)		
Biases		
Body language		

7. Do you notice any personality conflicts between participants? If so, how do they affect the negotiations?

8. Has any firm decision been made?

9. If a decision was made requiring action, was it clearly indicated who should carry it out and when?

10. Do you feel that the negotiation was successful? Why (or why not)? Did it fulfil the stated objective?

11. Did you observe particular skills or practices that you would like to incorporate into your own negotiations in future? What are they?

12. Did you observe any lapses or problems you think could have been avoided? How would you have dealt with them?

13. If the negotiation involved participants with whom you may one day negotiate, did you notice any style or pattern in their behaviour that could be of use to you in the future?

We have pinpointed the key things to consider when planning a negotiation. Observing a negotiation at first hand and filling in this worksheet should have helped to concentrate your mind wonderfully. Now you should be ready to enter into your own negotiation, but first make absolutely sure that you do have a good case to make, one that will stand up to fierce opposition. Furthermore, thinking it right through, have you anticipated what its consequences will be, win or lose?

Just in case you do have some lingering doubts, either about the substance of your case or timing, fill out the following worksheet before you finally commit yourself to a negotiation.

WORKSHEET 11

Are You Ready to Negotiate?

1. Identify the problem or situation you wish to negotiate about.
   i.   What is the key issue for you?

   ii. Are there minor issues you wish to raise, or issues that may come up during the negotiation? What are they?

   iii. Have you considered possible issues the other side may raise, and how you would deal with them?

2. Has the key issue been raised before, either by you or a colleague? With what results?

3. Do you feel your request is appropriate, given the timing of it, the general working conditions in your organization, the money it may require and any other relevant considerations?

4. Will the request generate conflict?
   i.   Among whom?

   ii. Can it be handled? How?

5. Are you personally committed to follow through?
    i.   Where will you be afterwards if you fail?

    ii. If you succeed?

6. Have you done your homework and prepared all your facts?
Can you pinpoint resources you will need?
    i.   External (e.g., lawyer, accountant, banker, media):

    ii. Internal (e.g., documents, grapevines, fellow workers):

7. Do you need help from others for the negotiation itself? A
network? A team?

8. How will this negotiation affect your long-term relationship
with the other side?

Look at your answers. Do they indicate that you are adequately
prepared, or do you think you should do a bit more research
before proceeding? Are the probable consequences of the
negotiation worth it to you? What are the chances of success?
And are you prepared to live with failure? All these factors must
be taken into consideration.

Negotiating for promotion and a good pay packet

All the techniques and skills that we have described in this chapter apply as much to your own personal situation as to when you are negotiating on behalf of your company. It's strange how often people who can be quite tough on behalf of others find it incredibly difficult to speak up for themselves. Women tend to divide off into two different camps: those who dabble in negotiation only when absolutely obliged to, and the others, a minority it has to be said, who have worked out exactly what negotiation is about and are using it very effectively to climb the corporate ladder.

Gail epitomizes the first type. She started as a secretary with an estate agency soon after leaving school. After three years she decided that she wanted to do something more ambitious so she requested a change and was offered the job of junior negotiator on furnished flats. She loves this job and does it well, but now she would like to take on more responsibility and either run furnished flats entirely or move to another department to gain more experience. The trouble is that she is reluctant to take the initiative with the branch manager because she is keenly aware of the competition among her colleagues who are all men, and she doesn't like the idea of getting involved in office politics.

Ironically, her job is entirely about negotiating good deals, yet she finds it almost impossible to apply the same hard-nosed tactics to her own situation. Her problems have undoubtedly been compounded by the Suzy Lamplugh case: this young woman's mysterious disappearance while showing a client round a property has caused employers to become genuinely worried about sending out their female staff with male enquirers who come in off the street. But Gail, and others like her in the same position, must use their common sense and suggest some elementary precautions which should be used by everyone in the office so that the women don't feel singled out and, therefore, unfairly discriminated against. This is all part of preparing your case thoroughly before you enter into negotiation.

Trudy, an ambitious advertising account executive who is rising fast by moving from agency to agency – a typical progression in this industry – takes the opposite line. She bases her strategy for negotiating rises and promotions on a carefully planned system.

First, she does her homework. She makes it her business to be thoroughly acquainted with her own company's salary structure and if the information isn't forthcoming from her immediate boss, she has no hesitation in approaching the personnel department. It is sometimes difficult to get precise figures from private sector companies but government and large public companies have well-defined grading systems for their employees. For instance, they will often specify the upper and lower limits of salaries for given positions, or the different benefit packages such as health or savings plans, mortgage assistance, use of a car and so on, available within each grade. Trudy also keeps in touch with salary levels and fringe benefits being offered in other companies, doing this by tapping into the grapevine and also by getting at least one serious job interview a year.

Earning more money is not Trudy's only objective; she is also concerned about life style, location and the type of responsibility she gets in her job. She once moved into another agency at a lower salary in order to acquire specific experience in the fast food business which she wanted for her overall advancement. Questions like, 'What can I look forward to in this company?' and 'How much travel does the job involve?' become part of the discussion when Trudy negotiates. Some of the specific gains she has achieved include moving expenses, and generous expense accounts and club memberships to help her entertain clients. Although many of these perks do come as part of the job, the amount you get may well depend on how successfully you have carried through the negotiation.

Once Trudy feels she has all the information she needs she is ready to move into her game plan.

Step 1

'Prepare yourself and your presentations.' Trudy runs through all the facts and then gives herself a pep talk to remind herself that she is not asking for a handout. She has skills and abilities that are marketable commodities and she is asking for more money, or a better compensation package, because she knows she is worth it.

'Confidence is critical,' she says. 'You have to communicate your conviction that you can influence the situation and make your boss feel that you genuinely believe you have something to gain from the negotiation, not that you are simply arguing for the sake of arguing.'

Step 2

'Choose the right time to start the negotiation.' Trudy strongly believes in the art of timing. She takes everything into consideration from her boss's moods to the overall financial position of her company before she asks for a meeting.

Step 3

'Always ask for more and expect to negotiate down, but never put the other person into a position of having to say a straight "no".' Trudy points out that skilful negotiation depends from the very beginning upon keeping your objectives constantly in mind, while at the same time realizing that you will probably have to trade certain requests. For instance, if no more money is available, she may ask for extra holiday time.

If her boss makes counter offers, Trudy always asks for time to consider them, and arranges there and then for a follow-up meeting. Her basic rule of thumb is: 'Don't forget that you and the person with whom you're negotiating have to work together comfortably, so don't do or say anything hasty that could ruin your relationship.'

Each of us has our own needs and a different style. If you think giving yourself a pep talk before negotiating is a bit naff, then think of other ways to build up your confidence. If you aren't interested in extra holiday time, what other perks would you be prepared to trade for a standstill in your salary? The key is to suit your demands, goals and style to the general principles of negotiation.

What every woman should know about compensation packages

Those of us who haven't won the Pools must face the questions of how to get money and – equally important – how to make what we earn work to our best advantage. Here are a few useful tips about ensuring you get the most you can of the fringe benefits available in today's workplace.

1. When you are being interviewed for a job or when your compensation is being reviewed, aim to include benefits other than salary in the discussion. For example, does the company offer more than the customary basics like luncheon vouchers and an interest-free loan for your annual railway season ticket? What about a clothes allowance or a place in a day nursery for your child? The more women come into management the more pressure they should be putting on employers for these customized perks. There's no harm in asking. They can only say no but it will start them thinking.

2. Some packages include a company car. Details on leasing and tax are complicated and subject to change under different government Budgets. A car may make a difference of between £1500 and £2000 in your salary. Keep up to date with the tax liabilities and work out what is most beneficial to you.

3. Pension plan schemes are changing all the time and you should get independent financial advice to make sure you are in a good one.

4. Some companies offer loans to employees for mortgages. These loans may be negotiable and you should find out if they are.

5. Share option schemes and bonuses are available in some companies. Find out about them.

6. The consequences of investment plans vary according to the type of investment, so if you are thinking of entering one offered by your company, here are a few key questions you should ask:

    i.   Is the plan flexible enough to allow for changing investment trends?

ii.   What are the commission and administrative charges involved?

iii.   What financial advice will be available to you in the future?

7. Disability and health insurance are other perks you should investigate.

8. Every time you receive a salary or benefit increase, find out how it will affect your income tax. A small rise or a company car can sometimes mean less take-home pay. Other forms of payment may become more important to you when this happens.

9. You should include retirement and estate planning in your financial thinking. For instance, whatever your age you should make a will. To help you start thinking sensibly in this direction, ask yourself the following questions:

i.   What are my assets?

ii.   Whom should I benefit in the event of death?

iii.   How does the inheritance tax affect my estate and what can I do to minimize its effects?

10. At upper levels of management, financial planning and counselling services are the new perks. Make sure you ask when or at what level this becomes available in your company and take advantage of it.

11. If you are working for a large organization, see if you are eligible for an expense account for business entertaining.

12. Ask your company to pay the fees for any professional associations you belong to, and also for subscriptions to any trade journals you think necessary for your work.

13. Whenever possible, seek company sponsorship for conferences, workshops and seminars which you consider are relevant to your work.

We are not suggesting that you can reasonably expect to get all or even most of these benefits now, but you should be aware of them, so that you are ready to ask for them when you have moved up to the appropriate level. Some of them, like financial planning, are subjects you should be considering now, regardless of what your company offers.

If you are self-employed it is even more essential that you become financially wise because there is no one but yourself to look after your interests. Employ a good accountant to ensure that you get all the tax exemptions available to you as a Schedule D taxpayer, and regard the fee you pay as amply compensated by the savings he or she will have made for you. Seek out a financial adviser, preferably an independent one who will not sell you insurance schemes for which he or she gets commission.

If you are running your own business all the above applies, and it's also essential to have a solid plan for everything that relates to your business. Make sure that you are properly covered in areas such as business security, buy-sell agreements, partnerships, contracts, payments of premiums, key personnel insurance, life and disability insurance.

Women tend to assume that negotiating is something new and beyond their scope. They forget that many so-called feminine characteristics, such as being supportive, cooperative and making other people feel good about themselves, are invaluable qualities at the negotiating table.

Changing your attitude to negotiation can change your success both in the workplace and at home. Winning or losing may not be the final value of any negotiation, but understanding your goals and the skills by which you can accomplish them will bring you that much closer to controlling more of your life.

WORKSHEET 12

Your Negotiation Plan

Assuming that you have filled out the worksheet on page 160 and feel that a negotiation is worthwhile, set up your negotiation plan here.

1. State your objectives: 1.   2.

                              3.   4.

2. Summarize your proposal to the other party:

3. Choose your approach (team style, one-to-one, formal/informal):

4. What are the trade-offs likely to be offered by the other party?

5. Which of them will you accept?

6. What are your deadlines for concluding the negotiation? Can you recognize stalls for time — and other tricks to distract your attention from the real issue?

7. What are the terms you want to set for implementation (who, what, when, where, how)?

Summary

* Negotiating is something you already do every day
* Know your strengths and weaknesses
* Be positive
* Always set goals and plans

9

So What Went Wrong?
Making the Most of Setbacks

There's little doubt that winning is wonderful, but the harsh reality is that even the most successful career is bound to suffer setbacks. Very few people are winners *all the time*, and indeed consistent success may not be the most rewarding course. How otherwise are you going to learn, if you make no mistakes?

No matter how well thought out your strategy is, there are going to be times when it doesn't work. The failure may be 'due to circumstances beyond your control', to use a familiar British Rail excuse, or it may be because you yourself made a mistake somewhere along the line. The risk was too great, you misjudged the competition, you got your figures wrong – the potential for disaster is infinite, but when it happens, try not to dwell on it. Try instead to look for the proverbial silver lining; it will be in there somewhere and if you can develop a positive response towards adversity you are taking the first step towards turning it into triumph.

In her book *Pathfinders* Gail Sheehy compares the critical difference between women who are functioning in top gear and those who are less happy. 'Women of high well being', she writes, 'usually have confronted a difficulty, rocked the boat, picked themselves up, and taken the painful steps necessary to free themselves from what they finally perceived as a trap, self-made or imposed. This is the source of a good part of the euphoria of a prominent number among the happiest women. They gain a great boost in self-esteem from having taken the risk and having sprung themselves from the trap.'

When Audrey Slaughter started her magazine *Working Woman* in 1984, she was convinced that her readers needed examples of successful women to inspire them, so every month she carried a cover story featuring a woman at the top of her particular tree. Stockbroker, photographer, publisher, entrepreneur, chief executive of this, that and the other, Audrey had no trouble in finding suitable candidates, and, without exception, their stories *were* inspiring and sometimes quite amazing. Like Valerie Thompson, described as 'a brilliant natural trader' who is now a Vice President with Salomon Brothers earning well over £100,000 and able to boast happily: 'I haven't an 'O' level to my name.'

'Why d'you show us all these successful women? They're not like us,' bleated some of Audrey's readers. So Audrey featured a redundant catering executive who agreed to talk about her difficulties in finding another job, which she did – very positively – and found something much better in three months.

'They never talk about their failures,' these readers continued to moan. Not true, of course, but all these women had overcome the consequences of their mistakes – that was in part the secret of their success – so though quite prepared to admit to them, they weren't going to waste any time looking backwards.

Take, for instance, Mary Hommert, a personnel manager with a City firm, who was featured in the June 1985 issue. Mary survived a nasty moment in her career when she had handed in her notice to one company and accepted a job with another, whereupon the new company changed its staffing policies overnight and decided not to take her on after all. What was Mary's response? Sit down and cry how unfair it all was? Of course not.

'With massive determination,' writes the interviewer, Diana Eden, 'she embarked on a formidable campaign of self-advertisement. "I spent a lot of time going to employment consultants and I put a huge effort into marketing *me*." She then composed a very careful letter, unemotional and pragmatic in tone, and sent it out, almost like a round robin, to a number of companies. . . . I knew I had to make it extremely professional. I spent money on having it word-processed, and also on printing it on the same sort of paper as my CV.' Not everyone would

171

necessarily choose Mary's solution but her refusal to accept defeat was admirable and it paid off.

There is a hidden bonus that comes from triumphing over disaster that you only appreciate the next time you're hit between the eyes; each time you vanquish one problem you become stronger and better able to deal with the next one. The situations are not always so extreme; most of us spend most of our working days dealing with small problems which only become big and threatening if they are not dealt with promptly.

Harry Truman's famous saying, 'If you can't stand the heat of the kitchen, get out,' applies very forcefully to your working life. If you start backing off problems or pleading home responsibilities too often you will be identified as someone who can't take the heat.

Heather, for instance, worked for a national voluntary organization which does a lot of fund-raising for cancer research. Heather's job was to get out among the local groups and drum up support from them to run their own fund-raising activities in the community. She felt demoralized by the prevailing lack of enthusiasm among the members, not helped by head office's inability to supply any backup because of its own reduced resources due to government cutbacks in research grants. Feeling that she lacked the leadership drive or the staying power to conquer this difficult period, Heather resigned from her position and asked to be transferred to a back-seat administrative job. It was refused and she was out of a job altogether because the management had expected better things from her and didn't appreciate her lack of commitment. In their eyes Heather was no longer a suitable candidate for promotion or even employment in the organization.

Women who work extra hard sometimes feel very browned off because they don't appear to be rewarded accordingly. But if you have got this far, and you have read every page attentively, you will know that hard work alone does not make for success. An entertaining book devoted exclusively to showing women how to get on in a man's world is Betty L. Harragan's *Games Mother Never Taught You*. The way she sees it, the women who advance have 'learned to evaluate the component of hard work

172

as merely one element in a complex formula for getting ahead in the male-dominated milieu'. The same idea, more succinctly expressed by Lois Jacobs, another *Working Woman* 'cover girl' is that 'if anything is worth doing, it's worth enjoying'.

There is another very real problem for women as they move up the ladder. Because there tend to be less of them, they become more visible than is sometimes desirable. The spotlights are trained on them and mistakes that would be ignored or forgiven in a man are held against a woman. The woman who makes a serious mistake is often made to feel that she has let down her whole sex. This is, of course, utterly wrong, but until there are more women in high places it's going to be a recurring problem. There will only be true equality when mediocre women get the same chances of success as mediocre men. Meanwhile, this is yet another reason for networking; the comfort of sharing experiences with other women who may have had similar problems is very great, and can be instructive too.

Bouncing back from a mistake

As a group we have begun to learn how to handle sex discrimination in wages and opportunities; we are getting better at parrying sexual harassment and the only slightly lesser annoyance of the patronizing (usually older man) who is always figuratively patting you on the head; we are getting adept at financial planning and organizing our time; and we are exerting a very significant influence on management style in organizations of all kinds. There's no reason why we can't learn how to recover from our mistakes.

Often women are not given sufficient feedback or constructive advice when they do make small mistakes. This may be because their male colleagues or bosses don't know how to criticize a woman; they are terrified of hurting their feelings. 'God forbid, she might burst into tears.' Don't give your boss the occasion to say that. If you do feel the tears pricking, make some excuse to turn away, fiddle with papers or go out of the room until you have regained your composure. We must as a sex, learn to be less sensitive and accept reprimands more easily and without wilting or brooding. The quicker you put the memory behind you, the faster it will be forgotten by everyone else as well.

Try not to take things too personally or be touchy about what you take to be a slight. Always assume that it's not, an approach which will discomfit the other person if indeed they had intended to put you down; but if they hadn't, then you have saved hurt feelings and misunderstandings all round. If you are in a senior position it can often be even more difficult to accept criticism, and men are no different from women in this respect.

Authority tends to isolate you, as Kirsty, the managing director of a small but vigorously expanding software company, learnt to her cost. She was desperately sensitive to any hint of criticism so when her staff attempted, politely, to give her feedback on some of her policies, she reacted violently and made it clear she did not wish to hear. Fortunately, a good friend, a mentor from her previous company, pointed out that she was running the risk of alienating her best managers and de-motivating the entire organization. Kirsty knew this fault in herself and now, although she continues to struggle with the leftover feelings, she is learning to relax and develop a sense of humour about her job.

'When things are a bit hairy,' she says, 'I step back and take a long breath. Then I force myself to take a good hard look at what is going on. Even if it's an uneasy situation, I've learned to pat myself on the back for the good things I've accomplished rather than allowing myself to be traumatized by possible catastrophes. I just try to keep a sense of proportion.'

One way to keep from becoming preoccupied with a setback is to look at your batting average. If your professional contributions have been acknowledged in the past, one error isn't going to cancel out all your successes. There's a useful lesson from baseball which we could remember to our advantage: one strike does not rule you out. Here are some other survival tips for bouncing back from a mistake:

1. Accept that your professional image has not been marred for life. Do not, even for a minute, allow yourself to imagine that this will be a permanent black mark on your career.

2. Make sure that you understand why you made the mistake. Document the facts leading up to the error and review them carefully to ensure that you will never make the same mistake again.

3. If the mistake can be corrected, develop a strategy to deal with it. And be positive in your actions. Convince others as well as yourself that this mistake does not have any lasting consequences.

4. If the situation requires further analysis to 'clear the air', act promptly and come up with a plan that incorporates the following strategy:

Decide   i.   Who you should talk to
          ii. What you should say
          iii. What has to be documented

5. Inform all the people involved of your intended corrective strategy and then follow it through with them. Moreover, when trying to recover from a mistake, it's important not to ignore the informal system of communication in the office. Indeed, it's often a good thing to talk about your mistake with your fellow workers because it may have affected your relationship with them, and that relationship must be constantly reinforced if it is to remain strong. Don't exaggerate the mistake but remember that if it's a serious one, one can't just say 'sorry' once and expect it to be cleared up once and for all.

6. Unless the mistake is a minor one, don't attempt to cover it up. That will only make things worse, if and when it is dis-covered.

7. Don't procrastinate. Deal with your mistake, both emotionally and practically, as soon as possible. You will feel much better once it is out of the way.

Remember, *no one* is consistently successful. Making a mistake, or falling down in some way on the job, is not the end of the world. Others will only interpret it that way if you let them think that's how you feel about it. Positive determination, rather than control or perfection, can be the most effective tool for advancing through any organization.

Of all the pointers that we have offered for handling your mistakes, these are the most important: never procrastinate, always clear the air and never look back.

Resolving conflict

Boys have been trained from babyhood to pick themselves up, stop blubbing and behave 'like a little man'. They are encouraged to be brave, fight for what they want and take risks. Girls, on the other hand, are expected to play quietly, keep clean, look pretty and help Mummy. If this sounds exaggerated, just glance around and see what happens in the average family, even one where the mother is working. It's easier than one realizes to perpetuate these stereotyped images and the conditioning goes deep. It's also harder to unlearn old behaviour than to learn something new.

This conditioning has taught women to believe that they are only acceptable when they are 'good girls', the sugar and spice and all things nice of nursery rhymes. Consequently, they are predisposed to avoid conflict at all costs. Instead of meeting the antagonism head on and resolving it, many women are inclined to sweep it under the carpet and hope it will stay there. It won't.

Moreover, women dread being called names like 'bitch' and 'manhater' because they feel these labels threaten their femininity. Name-calling of this kind is a technique developed by insecure men for dismissing uppity women who don't know their subservient place. Hence, an 'authoritative' or 'tough' man will be a 'bossy' or 'aggressive' woman. Recognize this attitude for what it is – an expression of inadequacy – and refuse to allow yourself to be cowed by it. Laugh instead and make everyone else smile by hanging this wry little verse up in your office.

How to tell
a businessman from
a businesswoman

A businessman is aggressive;
a businesswoman is pushy.
He is careful about details;
she is picky.
He loses his temper because
he's so involved in his job;
she's bitchy.
He's depressed (or hung over),
so everyone tiptoes past his office;
she's moody, so it must be
her time of the month.
He follows through;
she doesn't know when to quit.
He's firm;
she's stubborn.
He makes wise judgements;
she reveals her prejudices.
He is a man of the world;
she's been around.
He isn't afraid to say what he thinks;
she's opinionated.
He exercises authority;
she's tyrannical.
He's discreet;
she's secretive.
He's a stern taskmaster;
she's difficult to work for.

NETWORK NEWSLETTER, Issue No. 6 (1987)

If you are aiming to take a leadership position in your job, this
will mean being ready to resolve conflicts as they occur, and you
must accept that sometimes you will be dubbed cold and

177

calculating – by people of either sex. You can't expect to be liked by everyone as you move up the ladder to success; you can please some of the people all the time or all the people some of the time, but never all the people all the time, nor should you wish to. As Thoreau once reflected, the problem with soaring is that the higher you go, the more rarified the air and the thinner the company.

Conflict is inevitable, but think of it as a challenge rather than a battle and you are already half way to resolving it. Far from losing your femininity, it is actually those female qualities of caring and conciliation which can be used to great effect in many of these encounters. Cast around among your friends and acquaintances and consider some women managers or bosses that you know. Do they fit the stereotypes of hard, bossy female or are they not, more often, warm, sympathetic women? You can be decisive and assertive and still remain an accessible, caring person. The one set of qualities does not cancel out the other.

Conflict should never be thought of as a win or lose situation. If you find it difficult to get on with a particular colleague, and have tried in vain all measures you can think of to improve the situation, better to face up to the fact that this is one person whom you are never going to please and just get on with your own job as best you can. If things become intolerable – maybe it is your boss causing the trouble – then ask for a transfer or look for a position in another company.

Where the conflict involves a subordinate – possibly a younger person who resents working for a woman – try first to have it out with them and get them to tell you what really bothers them about you. It may be something quite silly – an assumption they have made about you because of some thoughtless remark you let drop – but their 'confession' may clear the atmosphere. The same tactic – you tell me what you don't like about me – often works a treat with male team-mates who are baulking at letting you into their charmed circle. The 'outsider' who takes them off guard may also make them feel a bit ashamed about their behaviour. If you can manage to make them aware that you know what they're doing without rubbing it in, you will win friends in place of the enemies you once had.

178

We are not minimizing the difficulties facing many trail-blazing women. It is tough at the top, and lonely, especially when you are the only woman, possibly the first woman in a particular job. A lot of people will be jealous of your success and only too pleased to see you take a tumble, but remember our guidelines for dealing with mistakes. The same kind of frank, open approach helps in resolving conflicts. In a hostile world, it matters more than ever that women should bring their diplomacy and caring skills to the workplace. They are, naturally or by training, good at something that is desperately needed in all spheres of life.

Learning how to use power will also help you to handle conflict. Like 'office politics', the word 'power' too often suggests a disreputable, self-seeking activity that should be avoided by anyone who cares about preserving their integrity. If you think about it, this is an absurd idea. Power is essential to be a successful leader and that is what you are aiming to be as a good manager. Of course, you want power to satisfy your own needs and desires as well, but a good manager uses that power to direct other people to achieve, with her, a commonly recognized goal.

Sue Slipman points out in her book *Helping Ourselves to Power* that women who 'see the quest for power as nothing more than absorbing the careerism of men . . . fail to recognize that decision making has been usurped by men and used to shape society to meet male priorities'. Do men have any more right to that power than women? Of course not, but if we intend to change the present scheme of things then women must be prepared to seize power whenever it is presented to them, not forgetting that with power comes responsibility.

The first step for managing conflict successfully is by identifying the key elements which occur in most such situations. Here are some examples of common types of conflict, along with brief suggestions for dealing with them.

Occasions of conflict

1. When there are tensions or differences between the leaders and the led; for example, too many chiefs and not enough

Indians, or vice versa. This problem is very common in the leadership race, both at informal and formal levels. One technique for correcting such competition is to make the position of chairperson on certain committees a rotating one, thus giving everyone a chance. Another solution is to give various people responsibility for sub-reports. This means that many people get actively involved in a smaller part of the project, thus giving them a sense of being genuinely responsible for their share.

2. When there is a clash between two potential leaders. Again, as in a relationship, competition doesn't work all the time. A bit of give and take is required, and if you feel you have been doing all the giving, start taking – nicely but firmly.

3. When different departments or individuals within an organization have a different style of operation or conflicting needs. For instance, creative and accounting departments usually attract very different kinds of people, often making it difficult for them to reach a joint solution harmoniously. Here the best chance of resolution lies in the ability of a senior manager to coordinate their varying skills and input. She must keep the needs of the company to the forefront and make sure that the different departments produce their work on time and with as much cooperation as they can muster.

4. When a powerful group of people thinks there is only one solution to a problem and imposes it without discussion on its subordinates. For instance, when certain organizations were first considering four-day working weeks, some of them imposed rigid schedules on all their employees. As time went on, different employees began to voice dissatisfaction with these schedules. It was only after several options had been identified and negotiated that the intensity of the conflict subsided and the companies came up with more flexible timetabling. It isn't always so easy – sometimes there *is* only one solution – but whenever possible, alternatives should be explored.

Basic guidelines for handling conflict

We can't let emotional setbacks turn the clock back. Use this quick guide the next time you feel down about a conflict. Check your own actions against those recommended here, and above all, as always, take the positive approach.

1. Don't procrastinate. Deal with the conflict now before it gets worse.

2. Never lose your temper; try to maintain your cool at all times.

3. Whenever possible, correct problems internally with only the people involved. Do not air them publicly. Keep to your organization's style of handling conflict. It will save face for the company, for yourself and for others.

4. Build strong teams and alliances. In addition to helping solve current conflicts, they will be useful in the future.

5. Resolve the issues without massacring your relationships. Don't burn any bridges.

The skills of picking yourself up from the ground, accepting your limitations, accentuating your strengths, mastering the difficult and recovering from unpleasant situations are the major challenges remaining for women who are moving up to the top. Resolving the conflicts which arise from these challenges is really just a specialized form of negotiation and requires the same basic skills with an added dose of tact, diplomacy and cooperation. If you deal with conflict as you would with any technical problem – that is, coolly, positively and pragmatically – you will ensure a successful outcome for yourself and everyone else who is involved.

WORKSHEET 13

How You Handle Conflict

Ask yourself the following questions about a recent conflict or conflicts you have experienced.

1. What precipitated the conflict?

2. How did I handle it?

3. What were the positive aspects of the way I dealt with it?

    i.

    ii.

    iii.

4. What were the negative aspects?

    i.

    ii.

    iii.

5. How can I improve my approach next time?

Summary

* Mistakes are the lynchpins of learning
* Nothing, including mistakes, is for ever
* Deal with your mistakes promptly
* Be positive
* Welcome power
* Face up to the reality of conflict in the workplace

10

The Critical Path

Ask any group of women or men what it means to be successful, and you will get as many answers as there are members of the group. Since people differ so dramatically in their individual motivations and objectives, there are no simple criteria for measuring success. The real question is, what does it mean to you?

The measure of a successful life, said Freud, was to love and to work well. It's a rule of thumb that still stands us in good stead today. If you are handling both of these skilfully, that is to say, if you have successfully integrated your personal with your working life, then you are in control of what is known as the critical path. It's critical in the sense that managing this tightrope between your two lives involves constant attention and adjustment as you balance the competing demands they make upon you. It calls for flexibility and proper pacing; being ready, for instance, to take a break if the strain is too heavy. View such a rest not as a gesture of defeat but as a positive measure, crucial in preventing possible burn-out.

Achieving the proper equilibrium in life is difficult for anyone. Working mothers, who are still primarily responsible for running the home, face particularly heavy burdens which require physical as well as mental and emotional strength. It's essential that they include in their career plan measures to help them conserve their stamina and energy.

We have written at length earlier in this book about the need for women to establish their own effective personal support systems. While this is important, indeed essential if they intend to continue with their career, we shouldn't forget that most women are not in a position to buy in expensive services like nannies and housekeepers. Most women are working because it is economically necessary for them to work, and almost one million women are single parents, many of them receiving little or no support from the fathers of their children. The traditional nuclear family with father as breadwinner, mother as housewife and 2.2 children is a vanishing phenomenon and now accounts for only 5 per cent of the population. Since women bear and nurture the next generation of citizens, we should be prouder of our mothering function and demand more recompense and recognition from the State, on a scale comparable with Scandinavia and many other European countries. For instance, parental leave is now common in several countries, whereas the British government, despite a directive from the European parliament, is firmly resisting compliance.

In Britain the law regarding maternity leave is not particularly generous and it has even been retrenched recently. To claim entitlement you must have been employed with the same company for a minimum of two years and it must have ten or more employees. If you are thinking of becoming pregnant make sure that you know how your company's practice relates to the minimum legal requirements and use your negotiating skills to organize the best possible deal for yourself. It is very difficult for a first-time mother to know beforehand how she is going to feel about leaving her tiny baby with a nanny or a childminder, so if you have contracted to go back to your job try to negotiate as much time for yourself as possible *after* the birth. This will give you a chance to bond with your child and to establish a routine and recover from the punishing fatigue exacted by those endless interrupted nights.

Few employers offer workplace crèches or nurseries but if you think there would be a good take-up in your company for such a provision, then why not organize a committee to pursue the matter? Alternatively, if you belong to a union, ask your officers to include this as part of the deal in the next round of pay talks. If women don't start insisting on these provisions, as of right, they will still be moaning about their unfair lot twenty years from now. Should you be harbouring any doubts about the strictly ideological validity (from a feminist viewpoint) of pleading a special case for working mothers, read Sylvia Ann Hewlett's book, *A Lesser Life*, a horrific indictment of the current American system where there is minimal provision for working mothers. This is not the pass that women's liberation should bring us to, nor should it be the price we have to pay for so-called equality in the workplace.

Guilt, regrettably, is something that few working mothers can escape. The cult of dedicated, round-the-clock motherhood is deeply embedded in our consciousness. If our own non-working mothers didn't plant it, then kind women friends who have chosen not to work will make sure we don't forget about it. The debate about quality versus quantity, that is to say, *how* you spend your time with your children as compared with *how much* time you give them, continues. The studies indicate that the children of working mothers in many cases do better than those of non-working mothers and certainly do no worse, unless the family's financial circumstances are particularly straitened or there are other adverse factors. In the end, it's up to each individual woman to decide what is best for her and her family.

If you are lucky enough to be able to pay for help, then have no compunction about doing so and get the best you can afford. A trained nanny or a registered childminder is a working woman in her own right who has bothered to qualify herself for the job and should be treated with the respect you expect for yourself. The view prevailing among radical feminists that it is in some way demeaning to pay another woman for doing some of your household tasks is foolish and counterproductive. What you must realize, however, is that domestic delegation requires exactly the same thought, care and follow-through that you would put into delegating a task at work to a subordinate which we described in detail in chapter 4.

Sharing your problems, exchanging ideas and pooling your resources with other parents in the same position – fathers can have these problems too – can be a tremendous help. It's networking all over again. The Industrial Society and one or two other organizations are now running workshops for managers and individuals who are seeking to find new solutions for balancing these divided loyalties. If you are not in the appropriate position in your company, draw them to the attention of your personnel department. Sometimes companies simply haven't thought about these problems because their female employees have bitten on the bullet and tried to carry on regardless.

Whatever the choices you make – marriage, no marriage, children, no children – there are three basic factors that influence the degree of success an individual can hope to achieve in her career without sacrificing too much of her personal life. These are:

1. Goals
2. Personal circumstances
3. The needs of your organization

Whatever support systems, routines or networks you use, you cannot escape dealing with these three factors as you progress along your critical path. How you deal with them is your choice, but deal with them you must. Let's look at them in detail.

Goals

The critical path can be very bumpy at times, so having specific, realistic goals as concrete symbols of your aspirations makes the ride smoother. Goal-setting is crucial to your progress along it because:

1. Goals help you to maintain an active approach towards seeking opportunities for advancement. A careful assessment of what you are capable of doing helps to keep you on track.

2. Goals function like the carrot at the end of the stick. Having them in view often provides much needed energy to recharge your batteries when they are in danger of burning out.

3. Having both professional and personal goals means that if you decide to slow down at work to balance some personal matters, your sense of self-worth is not shattered. You have not

relinquished your goals. You have only delayed their fulfilment in order to attain other goals that are equally valid within the ambit of your particular critical path.

Here are some steps to help you monitor your goals so that they are neither too high nor too low.

Relate goals to your own assessment of yourself

This requires examining yourself – your motivation, your abilities and your needs – as honestly as possible. We all have a unique energy level and tolerance for stress, as well as unique basic skills.

Margaret, for instance, has worked her way near to the top of a multinational corporation. She has travelled the world on her company's business and has, by any standards, been a very successful woman. Recently she married a man fifteen years older than herself who was already semi-retired and made it clear to Margaret that he would prefer her to spend more time with him and less at work. They both share a great love of sailing and Margaret decided that she would give up her full-time position to work only three days a week on a freelance consultancy basis. They bought a house on a river where they could keep a boat and she does most of her work from home.

Many of her friends see this as a cop-out, not realizing that it was a decision Margaret hadn't made overnight or entirely because of her new husband; it had been a direction she had been thinking about for a long time. She had achieved success in one field; now she wanted more time for herself, and her husband. The point here is that you must tailor your goals to your own needs, not other people's expectations.

Some of us require more recognition for our achievements than others, or different perks, and these will help to determine what your goals will be. Isobel is a journalist who can't imagine any other more interesting working life. A restless spirit, she doesn't want to be tied to an editor's chair, even though she has proved herself once in that position and was recently offered a tempting opportunity to start a new magazine. Travel is her great passion and she is currently planning an unusual journey for a book, so she turned down the offer – and a lot more money than she can realistically hope to get either from her book or her freelance commissions. But money is not her main goal in life – excitement, new people, new sights and adventures are what matter more to her.

Each individual must develop her own career goals and the timetable for achieving them within the context of her personal circumstances. It is critical, therefore, that you answer some key questions. Your answers will reflect your priorities and your value system, which are vital in helping you to maintain your focus along the critical path.

WORKSHEET 14

Establishing Priorities for Goal-setting

1. Of all my roles (working woman, wife, mother, daughter, etc.), which occupy most of my time and energy, in order of priority?

2. In what order would I like to see these roles?

3. What are my strengths, both personal and professional?

4. What are my limitations?

5. What personal and professional activities do I want to continue?

6. What personal and professional activities do I want to stop?

7. How do I want to grow in my career?

If your answers to questions 1 and 2 are different, you may want to make changes in the amount of time and energy you invest in your various roles. Do your strengths and weaknesses indicate a pattern that can help you set your goals? If you have identified specific activities you want to stop, can you set goals to do so? All these questions should be considered when you sit down to set your goals.

Develop flexibility

Flexibility is crucial to managing the critical path. Goals give us a structure by which we can monitor our day-to-day lives, and although we would very much like to follow this personal plan for success, life doesn't always oblige. New opportunities emerge, new demands are imposed on us, new developments rock our comfortable boat. The key to success is learning how to cope with change and being able to readjust when necessary so that new situations can be brought under control.

This requires flexibility and a readiness to re-evaluate constantly your progress, rather than pursuing relentlessly one goal which may not eventually be productive. If you don't monitor your goals in terms of your results, you will lose any sense of whether or not you are making progress. You need to know when you have ended up in a situation where it's better to cut your losses and run than go on hanging in there trying to achieve the impossible. You could still be there when you reach retirement age.

Your needs will change over time so be ready to anticipate problems, alterations in circumstances or new events. Linda, for example, was a successful personnel manager and had every likelihood of getting to the top of her organization. However, she suddenly developed the travel bug so she took the risk of leaving her job for two years in order to go round the world. She never did return to personnel work but switched careers and became a buyer for a department store because of the travel opportunities it offered. She has never regretted her first career in personnel; indeed, it has stood her in good stead, but it's just that her order of priorities has changed.

Many people become so preoccupied by the goals they have

191

set for themselves in the past that they fail to see that they are no longer relevant. The framework in which you set your goals is very important, but you can allow yourself the privilege, from time to time, of shifting the goal posts to suit your new needs. As a reminder to anticipate new situations, here are some questions that should keep you on track:

WORKSHEET 15

Keeping on Your Toes

---

1. What future trends in your industry might affect your career plans?

    i.

    ii.

    iii.

2. What do you need to prepare yourself for such trends (e.g., further training, broader experiences, relocation etc.)?

    i.

    ii.

    iii.

3. What stressors or changes do you see in your personal life in the next year?

4. What plans should you be making to accommodate these changes?

5. Are these plans compatible with your other goals? If not, how can you make them compatible? Or should you rethink that first lot of goals?

Personal circumstances

The reality of your personal life, your relationships, and the changing circumstances over which you don't always have complete control, will influence your decisions about the way you wish to conduct your life and your career. Each of us is unique and what is right for one person may not be right for another. To help you examine your individual needs and help you to make the right decisions for you, we have suggested some things you should be thinking about.

Setting your own pace

What might seem to be the best career decision in the world will not work out if it doesn't mesh with your personal life. This is why it's important to climb the ladder according to your own timetable. However, you must also recognize that your own clock is influenced by its interaction with those of others who are significant in your life.

Consider, for instance, that your partner, your children or your parents may need special attention for a period of time. Or there may be an offer of promotion involving relocation for either you or your partner. How are you going to resolve the dilemma? You may want to take a career break to start a family, but you feel concerned that it's going to affect your future advancement. Or you may worry that your biological clock is ticking away inexorably and if you don't have a child soon it will be too late, yet you are reluctant to give up your independence to live with the putative child's father. But will you be able to cope as a single mother, financially and emotionally? If married women need good support systems, how much more so the single woman who decides to take on a responsibility of this nature.

Not surprisingly, these are the kind of problems which many working women find difficult to handle. The pressure to change working practices is beginning to make itself felt; for example, some companies are becoming much more helpful about relocation, and, if it is absolutely necessary for one partner, the other will be helped with counselling and practical information to find a new position. However, until this type of practice becomes much more common, women – and the growing numbers of men who want more participation in their family life – will continue to find it difficult to reconcile the conflicting demands. Remember what we said about stress earlier and avoid overburdening yourself. If there are major family problems, a change in your working life, even if it is for the better, may have to be deferred, or given up.

In some companies, women simply do not move into managerial positions as quickly as men. Other companies do not have overtly restrictive policies but in practice they still adhere to the old stereotypes: women are often judged on qualities such as prettiness or pleasantness rather than on their performance as professionals.

Sometimes, the fault lies with women themselves. The real problem is not an externally imposed block to advancement but the fact that the individual hasn't worked out how to create her own route to success. This is particularly true of women who carry a lot of psychological baggage, not the lightest of which is their unadmitted fear of independence.

This is where the power of positive thinking comes into play. Remember the old adage that nothing succeeds like success. Knowing that you are driving your own car, that you have mastered situations you never imagined you would be in, gives you the energy and drive to overcome not only any reluctance you may have in stepping forward, but often the lingering corporate resistance to promoting women. Use your conviction and positive attitude to convince your employers that you can do the job, and be guided by your practical good sense to determine the pace at which you want to move.

Your business preferences

As our perception of success is very subjective, so too are our aspirations. Whether you would be better self-employed or working in a large company or a small business is a question that you will have to answer according to your own goals, style and opportunities. Here's a brief overview of the different advantages each of these options offers. Which one sounds right for you?

Running your own business

The sense of having a personal stake in one's work can be an inspiring source of innovation, commitment and a determination to reach desired goals. For many women, this freedom and determination is easier for them to achieve in small businesses of their own.

Women, who have had the experience of working in organizations where they feel that they have been refused jobs they really wanted, or which were reluctant to adapt in any way to their needs, often see starting their own business as the most realistic way to accommodate their aspirations.

Many of the most successful businesses now being run by women were born in the kitchen or living room as ways of harnessing domestic skills to make a bit of extra money for the housekeeping. Vivienne Flowers and her pizzas, Anita Roddick and her Bodyshops, Laura Ashley and her dresses all started like this – and look where their companies are now. Women with entrepreneurial skills thrive on being their own bosses, taking financial risks and dealing in every aspect of their business as Leah Herz's entertaining and instructive book *The Business Amazons* clearly shows.

If you have an idea good enough to convince your bank manager to lend you some money; if you have done your research thoroughly to make sure there's a market for selling it; and finally, if you have enough energy and single-mindedness to follow it through, then you have a good chance of succeeding. But never forget that a business of your own, especially when you are starting it up, will take a lot of time. If you have a family or other interests outside work, you should think very carefully before deciding to go it alone.

Working for a large organization

Although there is certainly room for a lot more improvement, breakthroughs for women are occurring in large organizations every day. Individual women have become inspiring trailblazers and they do serve as role models for other women. Use your judgement and sense of timing to decide whether the opportunities in your company are right for you at the time they come up.

Sylvia is a manager in communications systems for a large company who has explored the possibility of moving to a smaller outfit. In the end, she decided against it because she prefers the larger organization for the resources it offers, such as a research department, library and a bigger budget. She also likes the fact that she can devote most of her time to highly specialized projects which she particularly enjoys. In a smaller company she would be expected to turn her hand to anything and everything, so she wouldn't have this opportunity to work at something in depth.

Working for a small organization

Generally speaking, small organizations offer women more opportunities to move quickly and get diverse experience. If the business is profitable, women can negotiate attractive work arrangements and compensation packages. Moreover, flexibility in work schedules is more likely in small organizations and this appeals to many family women because of their added responsibilities on the home front.

Lucy is a young woman working as an administrative assistant in a small management consultancy. In addition to her secretarial work, she also does the book-keeping, writes the press releases and handles all the telephone enquiries which often involves selling the company's services. She enjoys her job precisely because she is doing a bit of everything. She knows that if she were working in a larger organization she would probably be stuck with nothing but typing. This type of varied experience, particularly at an early stage in your career, can be invaluable for broadening skills and, therefore, possibilities.

Developing new scripts

Often, we simply do not recognize how many old habits are still plaguing our day-to-day lives. This can be a problem because the successful management of a career frequently requires us to develop new scripts. How many scripts we will need to revise, and how often, depends upon our personal circumstances.

Vanessa, for instance, is a family woman who has been working full time for seventeen years, but for the first ten years she continued to do all the housework herself. She describes those years as slavery, until finally she pulled herself up, realized she could easily afford a cleaning woman and that her husband was perfectly willing to do the supermarket shopping. She had been a victim of her own perfectionism, a fault to which women as a group are too easily prone, as we have stated more than once in these pages.

If we could dispense with the crippling myth that we alone must assume full responsibility for the household, then we would be able to give ourselves more time for *all* our relationships, personal and working. These old patterns of behaviour are really not productive for the world we are living in today. When we develop new and more appropriate patterns, we will be making choices that keep us in control of our critical path.

Nowhere is this more true than in our behaviour when it comes to power. In the past, women weren't supposed to have power, let alone exploit it, or at least not overtly. But as we move onwards and upwards in our working lives, so too our attitudes to power must change. It's another script that needs rewriting because, as we pointed out in chapter 9, until we are prepared to take and use power, we are not going to effect any lasting changes, either for ourselves or others.

The way you handle power for yourself will affect your management of the critical path in all kinds of ways. For instance, take the comparatively trivial case of scheduling holidays. If you are in a senior position and need to take your holiday between certain dates to fit in with other family obligations, you must use your seniority over other staff members so that you get what you want. If you are squeamish about pulling rank, you will find yourself bottom of the list.

Advancing through any organization is really rather like driving a car. You are in charge of the vehicle but you have to share the road with other drivers. How well you manage on the motorway depends not only on your good driving but also on how astute you are at anticipating what other drivers are going to do. In addition to watching out for them, you should also be reading the signs which tell you about the location and mechanisms of power, change, leadership and success. Being aware of all these factors is crucial to performing well and taking you on your way along the critical path.

Women who handle power successfully will find that their subordinates become more cooperative and willing to change. As team spirit is enhanced and you acquire this solid support group behind you, you improve your own chances of advancement.

Handling the costs and trade-offs

As the saying goes, 'there's no such thing as a free lunch'. If you want something worthwhile, expect to pay a price for it. And if it's success you are seeking, then it's all the more necessary to weigh up the costs and benefits carefully.

Many women have seen through the Superwoman myth and have decided that they would prefer to slow down their career advancement during the time that their children are young. If they are lucky enough to work in an industry where career breaks have been established they can return after a few years and pick up where they left off. Of course, they can't be completely idle during that break; the banks, for instance, expect them to keep up to date with new developments and spend a few weeks every year back at work. Other women negotiate a period of part-time work with their organization, thus easing themselves gradually back into the hurly-burly.

Some, like Rebecca who is a solicitor, take the opportunity to make a career change. After years of working in a big commercial firm, the birth of her daugher made her decide to leave the pressurized world of high finance and giddy litigation to work as a combined legal adviser and administrator for an inner city job creation enterprise. Her salary is half what she was earning before and she doesn't have a car or other perks, but her time is much more her own and she still earns enough to pay for the nanny and the cleaning woman so that she can enjoy to the full the time she spends with her daughter. Behind her is the satisfaction of having done very well in one career; ahead of her lies the prospect of forging a new one in a field which she finds is a constant challenge to her ingenuity and powers of persuasion.

A mother who chooses to remain in the workplace on the fast

track *must* organize an efficient, completely fail-safe support system; even so she should still take the occasional leave of absence to avoid burn-out. She should take full advantage of her move up the ladder and her correspondingly increased power to negotiate more flexibility in her working hours. Remember that we said your employer can be viewed as part of your support system.

Achieving a satisfactory life balance can be quite as difficult for the older woman whose children have grown up and left home. On the face of it, things should be easier as the demands lessen but 't'aint necessarily so'.

Penny, for instance, in her late forties, is running her own printing company with a staff of twenty-six. She loves having her own business and would, she admits, feel total panic if she lost it. Penny appears to be the perfect career woman – goal-oriented, financially independent and happily married. Not so, she says, pointing out that there are strains in both love and work. For one thing, it's lonely at the top. 'I'm the managing director and chairman, so who do I turn to for support?' she asks. She pushes herself to make contacts with women in the business world who are at her level, but says that it isn't easy to establish close relations, especially as they are chary of revealing too much about their own companies. Her family is very important to her, but though she gets on well with her children, her marriage is suffering. She feels that communication is breaking down between her and her husband and they no longer have much of a joint social life.

Penny wonders whether she is devoting too much time to her business at the expense of her marriage, or whether she is throwing herself into her work because her marriage is unsatisfying. She needs to look closely at her priorities and goals, both personal and professional, before she can resolve her situation.

The critical path is no easier for single women. The stresses for them may be different in kind but not in the toll they take. A single woman who is successful may get so wrapped up with her work that she doesn't have a social life. A constant round of business entertaining is not comparable. Everyone needs the opportunity from time to time to relax with friends and in an atmosphere which is quite separate from their working life. Or they may need to get away from everyone.

Lillian, a high-powered executive in a magazine publishing company, books herself into a health farm twice a year for a week. 'I know I'm paying the earth to starve myself but I'm also paying for the luxury of total self-indulgence. I take every massage, bath and beauty treatment I can and I come back feeling wonderful.'

Sex and the single woman can also pose problems. Women have been conditioned to be attracted to men who are more powerful than they are, but as the successful woman goes up the ladder she is going to meet fewer available men of comparable status and ability. Furthermore, some men feel threatened by successful women and shun them.

No matter what our circumstances are, there are costs and trade-offs to be reckoned with. As in setting your goals, you must look carefully at your needs and priorities before deciding what you are – and are not – prepared to pay for your career.

Personal circumstances play probably the biggest part in managing the critical path. The woman who walks that path successfully accepts that she must often leave familiar emotional territory behind. Only then will she be able to increase her options to develop the skills to cope with greater flexibility in her life style.

The needs of your organization

However carefully you think through your strategy for advancement, it won't be truly effective unless it fits in with the reality of your organization. Successful women are very well tuned to the formal and informal realities of their organizations. They plan the timing of their actions and they are sensitive in their dealings with their colleagues.

If you want to advance particularly fast, then you must also be particularly sensitive about the impression your ambition makes on others. You have to make some effort to reconcile your own fast track record and your desire to be in the limelight with the overall aims of the company and the needs of others with whom you work. Occasionally, it may even be necessary to curb your pace and pay more respect to the chain of command. You could be dancing too fast for the rest of the group.

Take the case of Eileen whose company had developed a new marketing plan. She wanted to be involved in its refinement but she had no intention of discussing her ideas with her immediate boss, the regional manager. She saw no point because he was not in a position to make the final decision, so she planned to take them straight to the marketing manager who did have this authority. When it was pointed out to her that this would cost her her present good working relationship with her boss, she reconsidered her actions. As it turned out, her immediate boss, who had always been supportive, was excited by her proposition and allowed her to work on a special experimental project relative to the plan for two weeks. If Eileen had bypassed her boss she would probably still have got the assignment, but at the expense of a valuable relationship.

It takes time to establish a rapport with your company and fit in with its culture. You will know you are managing the critical path well when you recognize that your desires may sometimes have to play second fiddle, for a while at least, to the demands of your organization. There is a difference, though, between temporary, short-term compromises and a sense that you are never going to be able to adapt to the organization. If you really feel that it doesn't suit your temperament or style, then it is better to leave. It may be a company with an excellent reputation but it may not be right for you. People often tend to under-estimate the influence that their work environment or their fellow workers can have on them, and how severely their job satisfaction may be curtailed if the atmosphere is not right. It's also very important from your point of view that the organization you work for should be capable of recognizing your capabilities and be ready to offer you the appropriate opportunities. There is no point sticking around indefinitely because you feel they 'ought' to give you your due.

The choice is yours

Early in our careers we tend to see our work as limited in possibilities by our training or the type of job we did when we first entered the work force. But with increasing exposure to new products, new clients, new suppliers or new methods, our horizons expand. We see other people doing jobs that bear no relationship to their professional training or previous work history. And we too are likely to begin to think of new opportunities.

This is a growing trend in the workplace today and people must adapt to the idea that they may change direction not once, but several times in their careers. The 'dare to change' theme is a constant topic in magazines and newspapers. In its February 1987 issue *Company* magazine featured six young women who had already made quite dramatic career changes, including a secretary who became a motor mechanic, a teacher who became a parks gardener and a nurse who was now a travelling saleswoman. These were not mere capricious changes of heart. Each woman had been properly qualified for her first job and was picking up new skills in the next one.

It sometimes takes many years – and many different jobs – to find out what you really want to do. Ileana left school at sixteen with several 'O' levels but no sense of direction. She became an insurance clerk, found the filing was making her suicidal, so gave it up and became a garage cashier, a breakfast waitress, an auxiliary nurse and a car cleaner in swift succession. Meanwhile, she was doing a part-time course for 4 'A' levels which she got in a year and this encouraged her to apply to do a combined degree in Philosophy and Sociology. Now, in her mid-twenties, she is working in a family resource centre helping problem families before she starts on her training course to be a child psychotherapist. Eventually she sees herself working in a child-guidance clinic or a hospital.

The moral of Ileana's story is that although her early working years seemed scattered and casual, in fact everything she has done has served her in good stead for her final choice. From the moment she was accepted on the psychotherapy training course, she has carefully chosen her social service assignments to broaden her skills and experience. For instance, she is currently helping a community group for women and she is also doing some individual play therapy work with children under supervision. 'I've had my eyes set on what I want to do,' she says, 'and I take any opportunity if I think it's going to give me the experience I need.'

The possibility of changing career midstream and taking up new personal options offers us many exciting possibilities. At the same time we must keep our eyes peeled for potential hazards. Initially, most women begin in familiar territory, but after the first few jobs major career decisions will probably take shape and these may mean striking out in uncharted areas.

Nowadays, it is encouraging to see that there are more new patterns and life styles; in short, more opportunity for women's self-expression, both in business and at home. More women are succeeding in business and more women are entering the professions – the law and medicine are both 50/50 now and we shall see the effects of this equalization in another decade. The future looks more promising than it has ever done before for women.

11

Looking Ahead

Before the advent of the industrial society, women made a very real and visible contribution to the family coffers by working beside men in the fields. But as industrialization progressed, the separation between the working spheres of men and women grew. The basic stereotype since then has been that men go out to work, while women stay at home to care for the children and the home.

In recent history, this pattern has shifted somewhat, most dramatically during the Second World War when large numbers of women moved out of the home and took over the jobs that men had left behind. But this dislocation was short-lived. The picture of postwar prosperity was a man with a house in the suburbs, two cars in the garage and a wife at home to entertain the boss and chauffeur the children around.

Now we have seen another major change. In most countries of the industrialized world women constitute half the work force. A major theme of this book has been to show how much our lives and, therefore, our thinking and our aspirations have been revolutionized by this change. What effects will it have on us in the future?

We are not futurists and we are not in the business of playing guessing games about what might happen. Probably the basic rule of thumb for surviving in this strange new era is to ground yourself firmly with sound values and traditions that you have tested and believe in, while at the same time cultivating an open mind and endeavouring to remain sufficiently flexible to make any personal changes necessary to meet new conditions and demands. This apparently paradoxical behaviour is actually a logical response to the situation. Your values will help you set goals and limits for yourself; flexibility and adaptability will enable you to adjust these limits.

If you think about it, you will realize that the first five chapters of this book are lessons in 'grounding'. They provide instructions in:

1. Developing practical techniques to help you plant your feet on the ground

2. Getting overviews of your work situations

3. Long-term planning for your career

The following five chapters, on the other hand, were about the more fluid issues that become part of moving up, the issues that demand flexibility and innovation.

Remember Cathy, Joan and Sandra, the three women whose stories served as an introduction to this book? Let's apply what we have learned to their individual predicaments.

Cathy, you will recall, is a secretary in a multinational company. She is twenty-eight years old, married with no children, and basically she is working for short-term goals: good clothes, an annual holiday and running her own car. She has not yet started to think of her job as a career. As such she is a victim of complacency.

Here is what she should be doing.

First, she should be looking round her company and other organizations to see what types of women she would like to emulate. Once she has thought about the different choices available to her, both in family life and in her career, she should investigate the pathways her role models have followed. How did they get to where they are in the organization today? What did it cost them in terms of their personal lives?

If what she discovers makes Cathy feel more interested in the idea of pursuing her own advancement, here are a few personal tips to help her get started. She should:

1. Review the status of people who are in positions similar to hers within her organization and take note of how quickly – if at all – they have been able to move on to other opportunities.

2. Request an interview with her boss and ask him or her to tell her frankly what her strengths and weaknesses are. And ask for advice as to her next step.

3. Examine her particular area of work and see whether she could not extend her range of responsibilities.

4. Investigate whether there is a course or some further training, say for a professional qualification, which would improve her work and give her more credibility when she looks for promotion.

In the process of doing all this Cathy will begin to realize that she has a wealth of untapped potential which, if only she realized it, would make her working life much more interesting and fun. This sense of having something useful to contribute would be reinforced when she saw how appreciative it makes others of her services. This new, active stance is the first step Cathy has taken towards jolting herself out of her complacency and ennui.

The next stage will happen when she experiences a work crisis and realizes that she must do something positive to create a career out of what so far has been no more than a paying pastime. Because she is young, she has the luxury of time. For a while at least she can be a sponge absorbing all sorts of ideas and influences, having her horizons enlarged by role models she admires and becoming more in touch with the people around her. This will improve her confidence and when she feels ready, she should tell her boss that she is looking for advancement.

Although Cathy has youth on her side, it comes with a price. Her boss, being male, may assume that she will eventually get pregnant and leave her job. If Cathy really wants to continue working, now is the time to make that clear. Complacency has a way of deadening confidence, aspirations and, above all, the dreams that fuel the will to advance. Cathy will have to learn to dream.

Then there is Joan, fifty-two and facing a very different dilemma. Her husband is on the point of retirement and he wants her to spend more time at home with him. When she went back to work ten years ago it was to contribute to the expenses of a growing family. That money is longer needed but she now enjoys her job. What is more, a promotion, involving more responsibility and commitment, is in the offing. What should she do?

Joan's problem is that she tends to perceive everything she does as being fixed and permanent, even inevitable. She imagines that because she is now middle-aged, the job she has is the one she will be doing for the rest of her life and that no further changes are possible. Consequently, she sees this new decision as an either/or question loaded with lasting consequences. Although she is very tempted by the offer she wonders if she is being disloyal to her husband and neglectful to her family responsibilities; yet the family are all grown up and independent, her husband is fit and active.

Instead of approaching her promotion as if it were a lifelong commitment, Joan should look at it as something interesting to do for a few years until ... who knows? ... she and her husband decide to move or perhaps take up some kind of joint retirement activity. One thing is certain: if Joan lets this opportunity go, she is unlikely to get another one as good. She has spent ten years building up to this point. What a pity to let it go now just because of some rather rigid ideas about family responsibility. This is what it means to be flexible about managing your critical path.

Sandra is the last candidate. She is suffering frustration because, although she has always seen her work as being long-term, she doesn't want to deal with the office politics and competition of top management. In a very real way, she is fighting her own fear of success: she doesn't, for instance, want to isolate herself from her staff or friends. All this leads her to think that maybe she should stay where she is? What should she do?

In actual fact, Sandra has already made more changes and learned more than she knows. She has been single for some time, she has experienced independence, she has become accustomed to enjoying money and what it can buy. Sandra really has to recognize that office politics simply involve another kind of learning; they are about communicating and interacting. If she can throw away her old script and learn how to play politics, she could be at the top for a long time. She must also be more willing to use her family and friends as part of her support system.

To overcome her fear of success, Sandra should look at each stage in her career as a course in skills training. Like many women at her level, she simply hasn't taken stock of how much she has already achieved, nor does she fully appreciate that she is a very different person from the young graduate of ten years ago. Women like Sandra have to look at how much their work has become a part of their lives and goals. Sandra is successful and committed to her job so she should take advantage of that success, instead of being frightened of it. Now is the time to consolidate her achievements and build further on them.

Sandra happens also to be suffering from fatigue. To continue like this could be serious. Part of managing the critical path is knowing when to step off it for a breather and this is what Sandra should do now – get right away for a while, stand back from her problems – and then come back refreshed before she makes any major decision.

One way of eliminating politics is to change your job but that is an extreme decision which should not be undertaken hastily. Anyway, no one can run away from politics for ever. It's integral to the workplace and will always crop up in some form or other and at every level. It's just that unfamiliar politics can often seem more complex and intimidating than the politics we know.

Sandra has mastered the basics of success. She has become efficient in financial planning, in negotiating compensation packages and other rewards within her organization. Now she has to work on the next stage. She must learn to acquire a public identity and live comfortably within it.

Active career women who are moving up today are moving into previously uncharted terrain, and the effect of our mass infiltration into the workplace has not yet been documented. There are, however, at least six areas in which both women and their employers will have to make adjustments before this unfamiliar territory is claimed by women. These areas are:

1. Self-marketing
2. Developing political style
3. Successful working relationships between men and women
4. Mastering the new technology

5. Personal wellbeing

6. Cultural changes and patterns at work

We have already dealt with some of these topics in a general way. Let's look at each of them now with an eye to the next few years.

Self-marketing

Conventional wisdom often suggests that selling yourself and your skills is in poor taste. Nothing can be further from the truth, particularly for women. Few rewards come easily to the second sex in our male-dominated society. Women will only obtain advancement when they have 'sold' their talents to their employers – and to society as a whole.

The success of any marketing strategy depends upon understanding the customer's needs and what he is prepared to pay, and adjusting the presentation accordingly. This applies equally to work situations, but here the difference is that you must learn to think of yourself as the product that is being sold and of your company as the customer.

Before you market the product you analyse its benefits; to use the jargon, you define its unique selling point (USP). In your case, it's your talent, your skills, your experience and your personality. How do they differ from what is commonly available? Why are they better? What can you offer your company that it won't find in anyone else?

The importance of knowing your own value and how to market it has never been more important than in these times of uncertainty and high unemployment. The weak, the timid, and the modest are the first to go to the wall when it's a question of survival.

Consider the following story, typical of many in these recessionary times. A chemical company was obliged to reduce its research budget quite drastically, necessitating staff reductions. Two jobs were eliminated entirely and one other was scheduled to be assigned to another department. Most of the people whose jobs were on the line sat and waited helplessly, with the exception of one researcher, Florence, who had enough political nous to realize that her survival depended on more than turning in a good performance. She made a point of presenting herself and her talents in terms broad enough to secure her a position as a candidate for reassignment. At the interview Florence was able to talk convincingly about her suitability for the other department and as a result of this self-promotion she got the job.

If you are selling your services outside your organization, it's important to know as much as possible about your clients' style of operation as about the criteria they apply for making decisions and key purchases. Some take longer than others. Many have strict methods and policies. You need all the information you can gather so that you can tailor-make your presentations and follow-up. And in your self-marketing, never forget how important it is to nourish your long-term relationships. These are the friendly 'contacts' you can call on when you need information or want an introduction. Such relationships offer a natural flow of repeat exposure and business.

For all these reasons, and because women tend to be too self-effacing, self-marketing is an area of expertise which they must develop and improve in the coming years.

Developing political style

In the earlier chapters we talked about getting to enjoy office politics – 'playing the game'. The next step is not only to play the game very well but also to develop a unique political style of your own. So doing will suit women who love their work; they may be upset from time to time by setbacks, but they prefer to tackle their problems head on rather than retreat wingeing. These are the women who want to win but who remain capable of having a good laugh, sometimes at their own expense. They get a kick out of standing back and watching themselves perform according to the new scripts they have written for themselves.

Just because of their past socialization, women, as a group, do, and will continue to have, certain unique political strengths. Usually they are much quicker than men in picking up nuances, such as non-verbal communication, and they are more flexible

211

about the roles they can adopt. A woman who demonstrates a good political style will use her natural talents – humour, sensitivity, an ability to focus discussion, etc. – to influence her colleagues positively. This is where being a woman has definite advantages – charm, consideration, tact and a warm, sympathetic personality are very acceptable female attributes.

Successful working relationships between men and women

Since men and women must work together it's important that in the future we don't end up with two solitudes: a male and a female culture in the workplace. Men and women must reconcile any differences or misconceptions they may have about each other and learn to see themselves as members of the same team. In the long run, custom and practice are more likely to effect change than legislation, necessary though that has proved to be.

Many men are still dragging their feet. They see women as threats to their power and they are in no mood to extend the magnanimous palm of equality. They rightly guess that power shared is power halved; it is also responsibility halved – which for many men would be a great relief – but as yet they are prepared to cede as little as possible. They have structured the workplace to suit themselves and they resent the idea of opinionated women coming in and maybe telling them where they have gone wrong. These are gut level reactions which go on inside companies among individuals, but overall strategic planning for the future demands quite a different approach.

It simply doesn't make economic or any other kind of sense, as Baroness Nancy Seears has been saying for years, to have half the brains of the country locked up in female heads and not to make proper use of them. The situation is changing. More girls are going into further education and training. On average they get better results than boys in their school exams and they are becoming much more career minded. If they are given the same opportunities as the boys they will make equally good use of them.

Organizations that are promoting an equal opportunities

policy do it out of enlightened self-interest, not because they are interested in justice. They are finding that it pays them excellent dividends in terms of acquiring more skilled people, and for retaining those women to whom they have given an expensive training. It costs, for instance, about £20,000 to train an engineer and these professionals are in desperately short supply, so many of the major engineering companies are now offering excellent career-break terms to their young married women employees who want to start a family. The actual time that committed working women now take for a career break has been reduced to three years which, in a lifetime perspective, is not much more than a blink.

However, it's not enough for companies to express good intentions by simply issuing booklets about their policies to their employees. A firm, convincing example of determination to see them through must come from the top; line managers must understand it's part of their managerial job to carry out this policy; the practices themselves should be reviewed and tested continually. Equal Opportunity officers are now being appointed in many companies and slowly the climate is improving, though it continues to be hard for a lone woman in a very traditionally male area.

Yvonne Barton, for instance, at the time of her interview for *Working Woman* (February 1985) was the only female geotechnical engineer employed by BP. She is a specialist in soil mechanics and the major part of her working experience has been designing foundations for oil drilling platforms. She may spend weeks offshore on a drilling rig and most of her working hours are spent in a macho environment. 'Experience and growing older', she says (she is only 30 now), 'have made the occasional skirmishes in the male/female battle zone that much easier to handle . . . I try to be true to myself. I don't put on pretences or the little woman act. I'm around to do a job of work.'

As more women like Yvonne move into these male worlds and prove their worth, the adversarial element will begin to diminish. The bottom line, after all, for any organization is development and increased profits, and they will only achieve that if they capitalize on *all* their available human resources.

Mastering the new technology

The challenge of keeping up with new developments in any area is very real. Each one of us has a different learning capacity and a different rate of progress. However, understanding and using the new technology is a must for anyone wishing to make their mark in the workplace of the future.

In every field the microcomputer and word processor have become essential day-to-day tools for general communication, as well as for more specialized functions such as projection of budgets and trends. This book, for instance, was written on a word processor which meant that it could be done much faster and the drudgery of retyping corrected drafts was entirely eliminated.

There are plenty of computing courses available (see Resources for recommended organizations) and women should have no hesitation in plunging into this area. Far from being frightening, it's totally fascinating and you don't have to be a mathematical genius to know how to use computer software. The potential benefits of using the microcomputer extend far beyond cutting down on clerical work. In management, computerization is used to make long-term projections, assimilate and record data, plan budgets – you name it, the computer can do it. *But*, it can't do anything without instructions from its human boss; computers are our tools, we must not become their slaves. This is particularly important for women to remember because, if we are not careful, we could be pushed into becoming a new kind of slave – the computer operative who merely carries out someone else's instructions. This is a trend to beware of, and a fate to resist at all costs.

Whatever level you are working at, the new technology is going to affect you in the future so get acquainted with it now.

Your personal wellbeing

While success is still the destination for which women are headed, the journey may take a slightly different route in future years. The workaholic life style associated with career success is currently the trend, but its costs are increasingly apparent. In this respect, women could bring to bear a wholesome influence on the work scene. Instead of determining to beat men at their own game, they should fight on behalf of themselves and their sisters to establish a more relaxed, less driven mode of work. Of course, there are bound to be times in any serious career when you will have to work under pressure, but watch out! Don't let necessity turn into a habit.

For many women, fighting fatigue is a constant battle. The never-ending pressure that women experience to 'hurry up' is caused by the overlap between career aspirations and private needs. Coping with this life style over the long term is difficult and that is why, as we emphasized in our discussion of the critical path, women will have to become accustomed to dealing with trade-offs. The challenge lies in constantly reassessing goals and balancing them with your personal needs.

Nearly all the women interviewed for this book talked about their attempt to achieve this delicate balance. They felt it was necessary to be strong-minded about cutting out certain stressors from their lives, and many of them were making deliberate adjustments to their schedules so that they could keep more private time for themselves to enjoy their leisure, their family life and keep fit and healthy.

This personal management is very important. Work at it through short-term goals first. Plans should be made starting with three- to six-month periods. Do you want to take a night course or set aside one night a week for a particular activity? Do you want to spend more time with your family? Choose goals carefully and realistically, and you should be able to achieve them.

You should integrate a similar strategy into your working life. One of the subjects of delegating to others and mobilizing their resources is to enable you to slow down a bit. Unfortunately, many women bring the 'I should clean up my house' syndrome to their office desk. Although a desire to keep yourself, your staff and your department in good working order is commendable, don't let it take you over to such an extent that you feel that it must always be done immediately or by you alone.

Managing your time well is essential for your sense of personal wellbeing. Learn how to prioritize your tasks and see what you can eliminate altogether. Forcing yourself to assign a low priority to certain issues and events is a good coping strategy. Above all, remember: you *must* leave time for yourself and personal care in the midst of your hectic working life.

Cultural changes and patterns of work

In recent years our thinking about the workplace has broadened to recognize that arousing people's motivation is a key factor for making them more productive as well as happier in their work. We each have to think about our own inner sources of motivation: the desire to achieve seems obvious but it is by no means the only reason why people feel motivated. You may enjoy the feeling of power your job gives you or the sense of making a worthwhile contribution, or that you are producing something useful or providing a new service. It may be that your pleasant working conditions, friendly colleagues, or the opportunity to broaden your social life counts for more than high financial rewards or getting to the top.

Motivation in any guise is the energy which makes the wheels of work go round, but it is only too easy to demotivate people. Women like men need to receive support and feedback for the work they produce. And they will only continue to produce high-quality work if they feel a greater sense of acceptance, recognition and economic security than currently exists in the workplace.

A reservoir of potential energy and good will is present in every group of women as well as of men. But if these forces are not directed through a sense of common purpose within organizations, they are unlikely to produce positive results. Instead, employees will feel that their needs are at odds with those of their organization, and their work will suffer accordingly.

The question of how organizations can remedy this problem in the future is already a serious concern. A recent survey of 470 companies, carried out by ACAS, the conciliation service, shows that companies who instigate formal redundancy agreements where compensation payments are above the minimum required by law, and voluntary rather than compulsory redundancy is the norm, enjoy better industrial relations. This means that they are more likely to win trade union support for introducing new technology and new working practices.

Interestingly, the same survey shows that companies now place a high premium on skills and consequently they no longer operate the 'last in, first out' principle. Yet the skills shortage in Britain is a continuing festering wound in the workforce and is the reason why so many of the current unemployed are unemployable. It has been described by Giles Merritt in a recent article in *The Independent* as 'the single greatest handicap to our growth and prosperity', and when it comes to industrial training and high-tech education we are, it seems, 'in a dunce's class of our own'.

The figures are shocking. America and Asia lead the world in their industrial training investment, America for instance, spending annually $40 billion whereas Britain spends only £2 billion. Europe trails behind and Britain lags even further behind countries like Germany, France and Italy. Our information technology sector is growing at half the world rate.

One shaft of light pierces this clouded future – women have a great opportunity to advance themselves provided they equip themselves with the necessary skills. In the electronics industry, for example, which is a key sector for any industrial country, women show themselves to be particularly adept on the shop floor because of their dexterity, and this is now being recognized with high wages and plenty of opportunities for further training. We don't need a crystal ball to guarantee that in the future and at all levels it will be the skills you can offer, not the sex you are, which will establish your worth in the marketplace.

Conclusion

More and more women are working and that's a trend that will continue, if for no other reasons than economic necessity. Statistics suggest that women are becoming widows earlier. Given current life expectancy, that means that many women are going to live one-third of their adult life without a man. One in three marriages now end in divorce and though remarriage is on the increase, the income of divorced people with children invariably goes down. Also women are less likely than men to remarry over the age of thirty-five. Unless women become economically independent, the shadow of poverty in old age hangs over them.

There is, however, another kind of woman who has come of age today. She has grown up, not only expecting to but *wanting* to work, and for her a career is not merely a means to financial security; it is a goal and a source of fulfilment in its own right. For these reasons, and we each have our own particular ones as well, we are going to be working for most of our lives. The purpose of this book is to help you work it out – to plan to make your working years the best of your life. You are the only person who can do that. To summarize, the message is as follows:

First, view your work as an essential, integral part of your life, requiring *planning* both short- and long-term. Second, be *active* in implementing your plans. Passive fatalism is your worst enemy. And finally, you must learn to manage the *critical path*. This is the most important and difficult challenge you will face, because it is a new road, full of unexpected ups and downs, turns and potholes. The integration of your work and personal life should be a continuing journey of discovery that enriches both.

There *is* plenty of room for women all the way up to the top. We know we have what it takes to get there; it's only a matter of time before we arrive. The day will come when career books for women are no longer necessary.

RESOURCES

Organizations

British Institute of Management (BIM)
Management Information Centre, Management House,
Cottingham Road, Corby, Northants NN17 1TT
Tel. (0536) 204222

Business Graduates Association Ltd (BGA)
28 Margaret Street, London W1N 7LB
Tel. (01) 637 7611/2

Equal Opportunities Commission (EOC)
Overseas House, Quay Street, Manchester M3 3HN
Tel. (061) 833 9244

Fawcett Society
46 Harleyford Road, London SE11 5AY
Tel. (01) 587 1287

Manpower Services Commission
Information Office,
236 Grays Inn Road, London WC1X 8HL
Tel. (01) 278 0363

National Organization for Women's Management Education
(NOWME)
Brenda Hale-Sutton
Hillside, Waterford Common, Waterford, Hertford SG14 2QD
Tel. (0992) 584179

Rights for Women Unit, National Council for Civil Liberties
21 Tabard Street, London SE1 4LA
Tel. (01) 403 3888

Women's National Commission
Government Offices, Great George Street, London SW1P 3AI
Tel. (01) 270 5903
(Free booklet: 'Women's Organizations in Great Britain')

Networks

(This is a small sample including many of special interest to women in business. Most industries and professions now have their own women's groups.)

Association of Women Solicitors
c/o The Law Society,
Law Society's Hall, 113 Chancery Lane, London WC2A 1PL
Tel. (01) 242 1222

Bristol Business Ladies Club
73 Queen Street, Bristol BS1 4JP
Tel. (0272) 299691

City Women's Network
Ferrari House, 258 Field End Road, Eastcote, Middlesex
Tel. (01) 407 8989

Network
25 Park Road, London NW1 6XN
Tel. (01) 221 8479

University Women's Club
2 Audley Square, London W1Y 6DB
Tel. (01) 499 2268

United Kingdom Federation of Business and Professional
   Women,
Pippa Ellis,
23 Ansdell Street, London W8 5BN
Tel. (01) 938 1729

Women in Banking,
Christine Solomon, Membership Secretary,
Personnel Department, Barclays Bank plc,
Fleetway House,
25 Farringdon Street, London EC4A 4LP
Tel. (01) 248 1234

Women in Engineering, Science and Technology (WEST)
72 Highbury Park, London N5 2XE
Tel. (01) 354 2492

Women's Engineering Society
25 Fouberts Place, London W1V 2AL
Tel. (01) 437 5212

Women in Enterprise (WE)
National Co-ordinating Office, 4 Co-operative Street, Horbury,
Wakefield WF4 6DR
Tel. (0924) 277267

Women in Management (WIM)
74 Cottenham Park Road, Wimbledon, London SW20 OTB
Tel. (01) 946 1238

300 Group
9 Poland Street, London W1V 3DG
Tel. (01) 734 3457

Women in Publishing
Lisa Tuttle,
1 Ortygia House, 6 Lower Road, Harrow, Middlesex HA5 ODA
Tel. (01) 864 1957

Women Returners' Network
Park Squares, Luton, Bedfordshire LU1 3JU
Tel. (0582) 34111

Women's Employment Project Groups
National Council for Voluntary Organisations, 26 Bedford
Square, London WC1B 3HU
Tel. (01) 636 4066

Women and Training Group
GLOSCAT, Oxstalls Lane, Gloucester GL2 9HW
Tel. (0452) 426836/7/8

Careers Advisory Services

(Some of these services concentrate on careers guidance; others
are more concerned with counselling; some also offer courses.
Wise to make thorough enquiries before you commit yourself.)

Career Analysts
Career House, 90 Gloucester Place, London W1H 4BL
Tel. (01) 935 5452

Career Counselling Service
46 Ferry Road, London SW13 9PW
Tel. (01) 741 0335

Careers Guidance Consultants
Hooton Lawn, Benty Heath Lane, Hooton, Wirral,
Cheshire, L66 6A6
Tel. (051) 327 3894

Career and Personal Development Associates
Mid-Career Development Centre, 2nd Floor, 27 Morland Road,
Addiscombe, Croydon CR0 6EA
Tel. (01) 654 0808

Careers Research and Advisory Centre (CRAC)
Hobsons Ltd, Bateman Street, Cambridge CB2 1LZ
Tel. (0223) 354551

Executive Counselling
Virginia Novarra,
2 Foxley Road, Malmesbury, Wiltshire
SN16 OBA
Tel. (01) 286 7995

Howard Affiliates Ltd
Karen Howard,
Abbey House, 128 Avontoun Park, Linlithgow,
West Lothian EH49 6QG
Tel. (0506) 842419

Independent Assessment and Research Centre
57 Marylebone High Street, London W1M 3AE
Tel. (01) 486 6106

Job Search Skills, Oxford
Heidi Flury,
39 Whitehouse Road, Oxford OX1 4PA
Tel. (0865) 249370

National Advisory Centre on Careers for Women
Drayton House, 30 Gordon Street, London WC1H OAX
Tel. (01) 380 0117

Options
Sarah Weston,
19 Belmont Road, Twickenham, Middlesex TW2 5DA
Tel. (01) 755 0133

Positive Action
Maggie Riley,
3 Milfoil Avenue, Conniburrow, Milton Keynes
MK14 7DY
Tel. (0908) 677387

Professional Executive Recruitment (PER)
Rex House, 4/12 Regent Street, London SW17 4PP
Tel. (01) 930 3484
(Register, free weekly magazine and 'Graduate Post')

Vocational Guidance Association
7 Harley House, Upper Harley Street, London NW1 4RP
Tel. (01) 935 2600/8017
(Also in Glasgow, Liverpool, Cheltenham and Northampton)

Vocational Guidance Centre
35 Corn Exchange Building, St Anne's Square,
Manchester M1 1LT
Tel. (061) 832 7671

Course Organizers

(This is a small selection of organizations that run courses in all types of managerial skills. Those of special interest to women are regularly listed in the NOWME newsletter and *Women & Training News*, both quarterly. Look under Organizations and Networks for addresses.)

Career Development Centre for Women
97 Mallard Place, Twickenham, Middlesex TW1 4SW
Tel. (01) 892 3806

Jobcentres in certain areas of the country. Ask at your local Jobcentre for details and free booklet 'Action for Jobs'.

The Pepperell Unit, Industrial Society
Robert Hyde House,
48 Bryanston Square, London W1H 7LN
Tel. (01) 262 2401
(Set up in 1984 to lead the Society's work of involving more effectively the skills, ideas and talents of women in the work force.)

Manpower Services Commission
Training Services Commission, Training Services Division,
Moorfoot, Sheffield S1 4PQ
Tel. (0742) 753275

Monadnock-International Development
2 The Chapel, Royal Victoria Patriotic Building,
Fitzhugh Grove, London SW18 3SX
Tel. (01) 871 2546

Speakeasy
17 Clifton Road, London N3 2AS
Tel. (01) 346 2776

Women's Computer Centre
Wesley House, Wild Court, London WC2
Tel. (01) 430 0112

FURTHER READING

General

Blotwick, Dr Srully, *Otherwise Engaged – The Private Lives of Successful Career Woman* (Facts on File, 1986).

Collins, Eliza, *Dearest Amanda – Letters from an Executive to Her Daughter* (Harper & Row, 1985).

Cooper, Cary and Davidson, Marilyn, *Women in Management* (William Heinemann Ltd, 1984).

Clutterbuck, David, *Everyone Needs a Mentor* (Institute of Personnel Management, 1985).

Dickson, Anne, *A Woman in Your Own Right: Assertiveness and You* (Quartet, reprint 1983).

Garratt, Sally, *Manage Your Time* (Fontana/Collins, 1986).

Goffee, Rob and Scase, Richard, *Women in Charge – The Experiences of Female Entrepreneurs* (Allen & Unwin, 1985).

Harriman, Ann, *Women/Men Management* (Praeger, 1986).

Henriques, Nikki and Hoskins, Tony, *How to Survive the Office of the Future* (Quiller Press, 1984).

Hertz, Leah, *The Business Amazons* (Deutsch, 1986).

Hobday, Jackie, *Women Directors – Who's Who in the World of Women* (Eurofi, 1987).

Huws, Ursula, *Your Job in the Eighties* (Pluto Press, 1982).

Marshall, Judi, *Women Managers – Travellers in a Male World* (John Wiley & Sons, 1984).

Metcalfe, Beverly Alloan *The Effects of Socialisation on Women's Management Careers* (MCB Univ. Press, 1985).

Miles, Rosalind, *Women and Power* (Macdonald, 1986).

Paul, Nancy, *The Right to be You* (Chartwell-Brett, 1985).

Robertson, James, *Future Work,* (Temple-Smith/Gower, 1985).

Rodwell, Lee, *The Single Woman's Survival Guide* (Thorsons, 1985).

Rodwell, Lee, *Working Through Your Pregnancy* (Thorsons, 1987).

Rossman, Marlene, L., *The International Business Woman* (Praeger, 1986).

Shaevitz, Marjorie Hansen, *The Superwoman Syndrome* (Fontana, 1985).

Shapiro, Jean, *On Your Own: a Practical Guide to Living* (Pandora, 1985).

Siltanen, Janet and Stanworth, Michelle, eds., *Women and the Public Sphere* (Hutchinson, 1984).

Slaughter, Audrey, ed., *The Working Woman's Handbook* (Century Hutchinson, 1986).

Slipman, Sue, *Helping Ourselves to Power. A Handbook for Women on the Skills of Public Life* (Pergamon, 1986).

Stead, Berte Ann, *Women in Management*, 2nd ed. (Prentice Hall, 1985).

Negotiating

Fisher, Roger and Ury, William, *Getting to Yes: Negotiating Agreement without Giving in* (New York: Penguin Books Ltd, 1981).

Ilich, John, *Successful Negotiating Skills for Women* (New York: Addison Wesley, 1980).

Training/Guides

Bolles, Richard Nelson, *What Colour is Your Parachute? A Practical Manual for Job-Hunters and Career-Changers* (Airlift Books, 14 Ballie Street, London EC14 0TB).

The Business Graduates Association Guide to Business Schools for Prospective Students and Employers, 6th ed., compiled by Professor Tony Kennerley (Macdonald & Evans 1985). From the BGA (see page 221 for address).

Faulder, Carolyn and Wallis, Margaret, consultant eds., *Graduate Working Women Casebook 1987* (Hobsons Ltd., Bateman Street, Cambridge CB2 1LZ). Available in careers libraries or direct from publishers.

Smith, Michael, *A Development Programme for Women in Management* (Gower Press, 1985).

Wickham, Ann, *Women and Training* (Open University Press, 1986).

Returning to Work: Education and Training Opportunities for Women, compiled by the Women Returners' Network (Longman Green UK Ltd).

Women, career-breaks and re-entry (1986). Available from the Institute of Manpower Studies, Mantell Building, University of Sussex, Falmer, Brighton, BN1 9RF.

Working Mothers

Apter, Terri, *Why Women Don't Have Wives: Professional Success and Motherhood* (Macmillan Press, 1985).

Blackie, Penny, *Becoming a Mother after Thirty* (Blackwell, 1986).

Coussins, Jean, Durward, Lyn, and Evans, Ruth, *Maternity Rights at Work* (National Council of Civil Liberties).

Hewlett, Sylvia Ann, *A Lesser Life – The Myth of Women's Liberation* (Michael Joseph, 1987).

Howard, Karen, *Managerial Skills, Yes, they can be developed in the Home* available from Howard Affiliates (see page 224 for address)

Kitzinger, Sheila, *Birth over Thirty* (Sheldon Press, 1982).

Purves, Libby, *How Not to Be the Perfect Mother* (Fontana, 1986).

Sharpe, Sue, *Double Identity. The Lives of Working Mothers* (Penguin Books Ltd, 1984).

Health

Cooper, Cary and Davidson, Marilyn, *High Pressure. Working Lives of Women Managers* (Fontana, 1982).

Livingston Booth, Dr Audrey, *Stressmanship* (Severn House, 1985).

INDEX

Nancy Friday

Jealousy

Why do so many intelligent, successful women get trapped in relationships where they are miserable, insecure and jealous? Why is jealousy so often the hook that keeps us in a relationship we would otherwise have left months before? Why do women's feelings about their best female friends so often include envy? And why do most men deny they ever feel jealous?

This crucial, unputdownable book, the result of a four-year personal quest, throws light on to every area of human relationships.

Fontana Paperbacks
Non-fiction

Fontana is a leading paperback publisher of non-fiction.
Below are some recent titles.

Armchair Golf *Ronnie Corbett* £3.50
You Are Here *Kevin Woodcock* £3.50
Squash Balls *Barry Waters* £3.50
Men: An Owner's Manual *Stephanie Brush* £2.50
Impressions of My Life *Mike Yarwood* £2.95
Arlott on Wine *John Arlott* £3.95
Beside Rugby *Bill Beaumont* £3.50
Agoraphobia *Robyn Vines* £3.95
The Serpent and the Rainbow *Wade Davies* £2.95
Alternatives to Drugs *Colin Johnson & Arabella Melville* £4.95
The Learning Organization *Bob Garratt* £3.95
Information and Organizations *Max Boisot* £3.50
Say It One Time For The Broken Hearted *Barney Hoskins* £4.95
March or Die *Tony Geraghty* £3.95
Nice Guys Sleep Alone *Bruce Feirstein* £2.95
Royal Hauntings *Joan Forman* £3.50
Going For It *Victor Kiam* £2.95
Sweets *Shona Crawford Poole* £3.95
Waugh on Wine *Auberon Waugh* £3.95

You can buy Fontana paperbacks at your local bookshop or newsagent.
Or you can order them from Fontana Paperbacks, Cash Sales Department, Box 29, Douglas, Isle of Man. Please send a cheque, postal or
money order (not currency) worth the purchase price plus 22p per book
for postage (maximum postage required is £3).

NAME (Block letters) _____

ADDRESS _____

_____

_____